*Enjoy the Game!*

# A SPORTSCASTER'S GUIDE TO
# WATCHING FOOTBALL

## Decoding America's Favorite Game

MARK ORISTANO

Synergy Books

A Sportscaster's Guide to Watching Football:
Decoding America's Favorite Game
Published by Synergy Books
P.O. Box 80107
Austin, Texas 78758

For more information about our books, please write to us, call 512.478.2028, or visit our website at www.synergybooks.net.

Publisher's Cataloging-in-Publication
*(Provided by Quality Books, Inc.)*


Oristano, Mark.
  A sportscaster's guide to watching football :
decoding America's favorite game / Mark Oristano.
    p. cm.
  LCCN 2008909609
  ISBN-13: 978-0-9821601-1-4
  ISBN-10: 0-9821601-1-9

  1. Football.   I. Title.

GV950.6.O75 2009              796.332'02'024
                             QBI08-600320

Front cover design by Weston Carls

10 9 8 7 6 5 4 3 2 1

# DEDICATION

To Verne Lundquist, who got me on the sidelines.
And to Charlie Waters, Drew Pearson, Babe
Laufenberg and John Gesek, who explained it
all to me.

# TABLE OF CONTENTS

A Word to the Reader.........................................................vii

Acknowledgments .............................................................ix

Who Am I, and What Can I Tell
You about Watching Football?.............................................1

One Play for the Ages Says It All .....................................13

Offense: What You Do with the Ball ...............................23

Halftime: The Ten Most Important
Figures in NFL History ...................................................61

Defense: Chase 'Em and Catch 'Em................................71

Special Teams: Where the *Foot*
Comes Back into Football.................................................87

Other Stuff..........................................................103

When You're at the Game...............................115

The Refs & The Rules...................................... 123

Post-Game ................................................... 133

Glossary ....................................................... 137

# A WORD TO THE READER

Many thanks for picking up this book. Just a word here to let you know that even though it's about pro football, most of the theory in here can be applied to college and even high school football. (At least, if you live in an area where high school football is a really big deal.) Everything just happens a little slower at that level.

If you ask pro rookies what the biggest difference between college and pro football is, they will tell you, "It's the speed." Every play in the NFL happens in a flash. Everybody is very talented. Where you may play against one or two pro-caliber players a year in college, you play against one on every **snap** in the NFL. That's why, for my dough, the pro game is the most fun to watch. (By the way, see how the word *snap* is set in bold above? That means that (a) it's a football term, (b) this is the first time it has appeared, and (c) it's described in the glossary at the back of the book.)

Also, even though most of the stories in this book come from the Dallas Cowboys and Houston Oilers, the two teams I covered in my NFL broadcast career, you'll get a lot out of this book no matter what team you root for. Even if you're a fan of the dreaded (CHOKE—GASP) Redskins!

And if you are new to the game, and you've turned here for a little help in understanding…try to remember at all times that it's just a game.

# ACKNOWLEDGMENTS

Thanks to everybody at Synergy Books.

And to my wife, Lynn, for putting up with all the
time at the computer.

The author is donating a portion of his proceeds from the sale
of this book to Children's Medical Center Dallas.

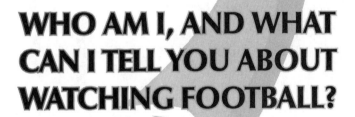

# WHO AM I, AND WHAT CAN I TELL YOU ABOUT WATCHING FOOTBALL?

# WHO AM I, AND WHAT CAN I TELL YOU ABOUT WATCHING FOOTBALL?

Well, I watched football for a living. I had a thirty-year career that millions of guys (and at least 346,417 women) would have sold their souls for. I got paid to go to NFL games and talk about them on the radio. Even though it's been several years since I left sports broadcasting for a career as an actor and photographer, I am still a huge NFL fan. I have the DIRECTV NFL Sunday Ticket® package, and I watch at least two games every weekend. And, as the old joke goes, my two favorite teams are the Cowboys and whoever is playing the Redskins.

And I've found that I watch football very differently from my "civilian" friends. I see things developing, patterns occurring and being exploited. And it's just a shame for me to keep all this inside info to myself.

If you're not a football fan but your husband/wife/brother/ sister/boyfriend/girlfriend/work friend is, and you feel like you're missing out on all the fun on Sunday/Monday/Thursday, then this book is for you.

Aside: Throughout this book, in order to save paper, I'll refer to the husband/wife/brother/sister/boyfriend/girlfriend/work-friend as the "Fan in your life."

Football, especially NFL football, is a fascinating game; it's chess played with human pieces. Something that you do in the first **quarter** is designed to set up something in the fourth quarter. Three plays you run to the left set up the play to the right that breaks for a **touchdown** (or "TD").

You can benefit from my experience as I demystify this very complex game for you. This demystification will be done not as a coach or former player would do it—with an overreliance on the subtle complexities it takes years to be able to recognize—but with the slightly above-average stuff you learn hanging around the NFL for thirty years. When you've finished my book, you won't be ready to coach the Colts or buy the Bucs, but you'll get a lot more enjoyment out of America's favorite sport.

So, who is this book for?

- If you're a rabid follower of the NFL **draft**, go away.
- If you live and die for the NFL **Scouting Combine** and you recap forty-yard dash times with your co-workers around the water cooler, find another book to read.
- If you're into fantasy football, you probably know more than is healthy; go back to your virtual roster.
- If you can't be interested in a game unless you have a bet on it, you're not a football fan, you're a gambling addict. Get help.

This book isn't for any of you.
But…

- If, like me, you believe that we should cheer like heck for our team on Sunday and then live a real life the rest of the week or
- If you'd like to learn more about pro football so that your viewing experience on Sunday (and Monday and Thursday) will be enhanced or
- If the Fan in your life is wrapped up in NFL football all day Sunday (Monday, Thursday) and you want to feel more like a part of the action or
- If you went to a **Super Bowl** XLII (that's 42 for you non-Romans) party and got caught up in the excitement as the Giants ended the Patriots' dream of an unbeaten season (arguably the greatest NFL game ever played), and you felt the excitement as Eli Manning threw that winning TD pass, and you want to know more about why things worked the way they did…then read on. Because I've got thirty years of professional pro-football watching experience to share with you.

# TIME-OUT #1

Pro football people are very funny. I don't know why. They just are. Maybe it's something about all those hits to the head.

Hall of Fame tight end Mike Ditka was a coach with the Cowboys after his playing days ended, and Mike was notorious for his hot temper and even hotter language. When his players were not the targets of his wrath, the referees often came into his sights.

Toward the end of one Cowboys game back in the seventies, I was on the sidelines, waiting to head to the locker room for post-game interviews. The Cowboys were well ahead, and the clock was running out. After a penalty was called against the Cowboys, Ditka took a couple of steps on to the field and, in an incredibly gentle voice, asked the ref:

"Excuse me, Mr. Official, but are you a member of the Fellowship of Christian Athletes?"

"No," the ref replied, a puzzled look on his face, since Ditka usually only screamed at the refs.

"Good," Ditka screamed, "because that was the worst g— d— call I've seen in my entire %&#*#& football career!"

Even head coach Tom Landry, notoriously stone-faced during games, laughed at that one.

## BACK TO PLAY

And just how did my fascination with pro football begin? Innocently enough.

I was a fourteen-year-old confirmed baseball fan, growing up in a New York City suburb. And one fall Sunday in 1966, with nothing to do, I flipped on the TV, where the hometown New York Giants were in Dallas playing this team called the Cowboys. Early on, the Dallas quarterback, Don Meredith, threw a short pass to Bob Hayes, whose name I knew because in the 1964 Tokyo Olympics he won the hundred-meter dash and the title "World's Fastest Human."

Hayes caught the short pass just behind Giants defensive back Henry Carr, and Hayes ran about eighty yards, into the Cotton Bowl **end zone** for a Cowboys touchdown, one step ahead of Carr all the way. It was the most exciting play I'd ever seen in a sports event. I was hooked. And it was with the Cowboys.

I began to watch NFL football every Sunday. Mostly, it was the Giants, a hapless team with no future. I longed for those Sundays when the Cowboys would be on. I wrote to the team and got a copy of the media guide. I lived for them.

From my teens on, my goal was to be in the locker room with the Cowboys when they won a Super Bowl. I reached that goal in January 1978, at age twenty-five, when the Cowboys beat the Broncos in Super Bowl XII and I was an assistant on the Cowboys Radio Network broadcast. In fact, not seven years after watching Hayes beat Carr to the end zone, I was interviewing Bob as a sports reporter for WFAA-TV in Dallas. Verne Lundquist, now the top college football play-by-play man for CBS-TV and one of the nation's best sportscasters, was at that time the "voice" of the Cowboys, and he hired me when I was twenty-one. (I had gone to Texas Christian University to study mass communication.) One of my earliest jobs was shooting sideline film at Cowboys home games. Could I be any closer to heaven? (At one point in my broadcast career, I was a weekend anchor in Nashville, Tennessee, with a very talented young woman as my co-anchor named Oprah Winfrey. I wonder, whatever became of her?)

I got to know Roger Staubach, Charlie Waters, Cliff Harris, Jethro Pugh, Mel Renfro, Rayfield Wright, Drew Pearson, Lee Roy Jordan…and on and on. And that led, in a somewhat curved way, to spending four years on the Houston Oilers Radio Network watching the one and only Earl Campbell week in and week out. The most exciting athlete I ever saw. The most punishing runner, the most gracious, humble person. And that led to an association with NFL Films, for whom I produced a radio show for two seasons, and also to a job working on one of the NFL's earliest computer stats programs. And finally, back to the Cowboys, and the Super Bowl team of the nineties, as an announcer for the Dallas Cowboys Radio Network, watching Troy Aikman, Emmitt Smith, and Michael Irvin go through their paces. In between there, I worked as a game-day assistant to the Cowboys PR department, and as a sportswriter for the *Dallas Cowboys Official Weekly* newspaper.

I picked up a lot of football knowledge along the way. From broadcasters like Verne and Ron Franklin. From players like Roger and Troy and Jason Garrett (Garrett could analyze game film with the best of them, which is why he's now one of the highest-paid assistant coaches in the game), and from former players turned broadcaster, like Babe Laufenberg, who parlayed a nine-year backup QB career into a great radio and TV life. From Charlie Waters and Drew Pearson, two of the greatest ever at their positions and with whom I shared many a game-day microphone. And from John Gesek, a former Cowboys offensive lineman who spent one year in our radio booth and gave me a unique, in-the-trenches view of things.

So, now I'll try to distill all that knowledge and throw some your way. When you've finished, you won't be able to immediately spot "Cover Two" or know which receiver broke his **route** off too soon or whether the ref made the right call when he signaled **intentional grounding**. But you will understand, for example, why first-**down** plays are the most important of any offensive **drive.** And you'll know what a team's first, and most important, goal is when they're faced with first-and-ten from their own two-yard line.

It's a great, complex, boisterous, imaginative game.

Enjoy it!

And, oh yeah, if you're some young kid who doesn't really have the talent to play football even at the high school level, but you have the gift of gab and you're crazy about a certain team…I hope you enjoy broadcasting a Super Bowl some day.

P.S. Skip over the stuff you already know. I don't want to insult your intelligence.

# TIME-OUT #2

The pressure involved in live broadcasts of NFL football can be pretty brutal. You're talking live, for hours, to a huge audience, whether on TV or radio. Of course, at the Super Bowl, it's the biggest audience of all.

Even though I was with the Oilers for the 1978 season, I was still close to the Cowboys Radio Network crew, and at the Orange Bowl for Super Bowl XIII (thirteen—those pesky letter/numbers!), I worked in the Cowboys radio booth. I wore a headset that was linked to the NBC production truck, so I could hear when the TV guys called for commercial breaks and alert the Cowboys Network producer.

There is a constant stream of chatter in the TV truck: director, producer, replay, graphics, engineers. It's moderately organized chaos. Just about thirty seconds before **kickoff**, I heard, through my headset, that the telephone next to the NBC producer rang. The producer picked it up and, in his gruffest voice, said, "Truck!" About twenty seconds elapsed.

"No, I can't deliver two large pepperoni pizzas to you!" And he slammed the phone down.

There were a couple more calls for pizza that day in the truck. Apparently the phone company had given them the number of an out-of-business pizza joint.

Unfortunately for the Cowboys, Terry Bradshaw and the Steelers did deliver that day.

The play from that game forever stamped on the memories of Cowboys fans came when Roger Staubach found Jackie

Smith all alone in the end zone for a sure touchdown, and the veteran tight end had the ball bounce off his chest, incomplete.

To this day, if I turn my head to the right in just such a way, in my mind's eye I'm looking around the plywood wall of the temporary radio booth we were in, looking down into the end zone and seeing the ball falling to the ground and Jackie Smith lying there in disbelief. That's how strong the memory is. That's what this game will do to you.

# ONE PLAY FOR
# THE AGES SAYS IT ALL

# ONE PLAY FOR
# THE AGES SAYS IT ALL

Think about the winning TD pass in Super Bowl XLII. (You should all know how to count these Roman numbers by now.)

It was a simple "fade" route run near the goal line, where the receiver runs a few yards downfield and then fades toward the outside corner of the end zone. The Giants' Eli Manning threw it to receiver Plaxico Burress over Patriots cornerback Ellis Hobbs for the winning score.

From the off-season, through springtime "mini-camp," through the heat of training camp, through sixteen regular season games and their endless team meetings and practices, and the earlier playoff games, it came to this moment. The final Giants drive of the Super Bowl, where the Giants, and especially Manning and coach Tom Coughlin, were striving to get a huge monkey off their collective backs, while the Patriots were looking to become the first 19-0 team in NFL history.

Even though the ball was dangerously deep in Patriots territory—the New England fourteen-yard line, to be exact—Hobbs gave Burress lots of room, playing almost seven full yards away from him at the start of the play. Hobbs was playing Burress "inside"; he was lined up closer to the middle of the field than Burress, allowing Burress to go toward the near sideline (away from most of the rest of the players) if he wanted to, because Hobbs thought he could pin Burress against the sideline, to prevent him from coming back to the ball.

At the snap of the ball, Burress burst forward, and Hobbs backpedaled, as they each had done hundreds of times before in this one season alone. But after only a couple of yards, with Hobbs at the five-yard line and Burress at the ten, Hobbs planted his feet and forced Burress to make a choice: Where did Burress want to run?

Years of instinct, film study, and training allowed Burress to realize that by planting the way he did, Hobbs was giving away the edge. Burress put on a burst of speed at almost the instant that Hobbs was applying the brakes.

Burress was three yards ahead of Hobbs at the moment he reached the goal line. Because the Patriots ran a **blitz** (sending extra guys to chase, and try to tackle, the QB in addition to the normal, onrushing defensive linemen—more on this later), Manning had to hurry the throw and tossed it a bit higher than he might have liked to get it over the extended arms of the approaching Patriots defenders. Ordinarily, because of the short distances the **offense** works with in the **red zone** (inside the other team's twenty-yard line), you don't want to toss the ball up too high—"put air under it" in football lingo—you want to zip it in there quick, so the defenders don't have time to get to it. Even though Manning took a bit too much off his pass and under-threw it, by the time Hobbs could make up any ground, Burress slowed up, came back to the ball, made the catch, and the Giants were on their way to being fitted for Super Bowl rings.

All three of these players—Manning, Burress, and Hobbs— had likely run this play in practice a thousand times. Manning and Burress from off-season workouts to whatever private sessions they had to perfect their game, to training camp, to the regular season, and through the playoffs. (They even came out before warm-ups officially began for the Super Bowl and ran it several times in the stadium in full view of the Fox TV cameras.) It was not a secret play. It's a standard pattern in every offensive playbook. It was a simple route for the receiver to run and a simple pass for the QB to throw, and the two of them could probably pull it off in their sleep. Hobbs, meanwhile, probably spent Super Bowl week lying in bed at night telling himself, "Don't give up the fade…Don't give up the fade."

One play, perfectly executed, in what may well have been the most exciting game in NFL history. (Of course, I picked the Giants to win, which is why I feel that way!) And though it only took some seven seconds to execute, it was the culmination of years of training among men who, when the training began, may not have even known the others existed.

It was a play that worked the way it did because of what those three men did, because of what the other nineteen players on the field did, because of what the coaches did, because of what the game officials didn't do, and on and on.

It's a brief illustration of the fascinating, chess-like aspect of NFL football. How you may know what's coming, and still be powerless to stop it. How you can make your opponent think one thing, and then do another. How sometimes it's about the brilliance of a coach who thinks of everything from every angle, and sometimes how the odd shape of the ball leads to the funniest bounces and craziest outcomes.

If you weren't all that good at geometry in high school, you may not know that the actual shape of the football is described as a "prolate spheroid." Trust me. It is. So, when your team loses a **fumble** after the ball has taken several maddening bounces around the turf, take a long hit from your drink and then, in your most melodramatic voice, say, "Ah, the unpredictable bounding of the prolate spheroid." Or, if you're not quite that dramatic, simply make the time-honored observation that, "The football does, indeed, take funny bounces."

As I've already noted, football is an amazing, endlessly fascinating game, and the good news is it's not nearly as difficult as it might seem to become a knowledgeable fan. You may not understand what it means if you hear the quarterback say "Brown right, slot right, max middle, pull forty-six, strong out go, on three" in the huddle. And they say it all so quickly it sounds like "browrighslotrighmaxmidlefortysixrongotgoon-three." And if you happen on a lost playbook on the crosstown bus, the diagrams and all will look like so much Greek. In fact, during Tom Landry's days as Cowboys coach, there was actually Latin in the playbook. Each play had a *sine qua non*—meaning, I think, "here's what you do if everything else goes crazy."

But I know you: you don't need to know what the quarterback is saying or how to read a playbook. Your goal is just to be able to sit in front of the tube on SMT (Sunday, Monday, Thursday) and have a greater appreciation for the strategy and the on-field machinations. You want to enjoy, and discuss, the Game with the Fan in your life. And while it's a complex game, you can learn a lot just by watching! And reading!

And, truth be told, the Fan in your life may pretend to know a great deal about the game, but deep down inside, they know that they don't know as much as they think they know. So, once you've digested all this and begun watching the games with your significant other, you might want to leave this book lying around for them to find. Or—better still—have them buy a copy of their own!

For now, let's buckle those chin straps and get to work!

But first, this important word...

# TIME-OUT #3

One of the most intelligent, informative, and hysterical people I ever worked with in the booth was Babe Laufenberg. Babe was a quarterback with nine NFL seasons under his belt, mostly as a backup. He has a Super Bowl ring from his time with the Redskins. And for my money, there is nobody better at explaining the game to the layman over the radio than Babe.

He often refers to a career in the NFL as "the world's longest job audition," because he knows firsthand that players have to prove themselves worthy of the job every week, before demanding coaches, prying press, and screaming fans.

In my first season with him, 1995, he told a story about his rookie year with the Redskins, at a late-season game in St. Louis against the Cardinals. (Yes, young people, the Cardinals used to play in St. Louis. The Rams used to play in Los Angeles. And Paul McCartney used to play in a band called The Beatles. And if you ask me who Paul McCartney is, I'm coming after you!)

It was bitter cold, snowing, and the kind of day that is horribly uncomfortable if you're on the sidelines and sitting still. Babe and several of his teammates were trying to get close to one of those big, cylindrical sideline heaters that kind of blows fire out the front to warm the bench area.

As the players watched the action on the field, a big offensive lineman nudged Babe and said, "Hey, rookie, your shoe's on fire."

Laufenberg looked down and, sure enough, he'd gotten so close to the heater that the leather of his shoe was actually burning. He stamped it out and plunged his foot into some snow to cool off. And what did he say to the team equipment man when he handed his shoes in after the game, all scorched and falling apart?

"They sure don't make these shoes like they used to!"

# OFFENSE: WHAT YOU DO WITH THE BALL

# OFFENSE: WHAT YOU DO WITH THE BALL

A t its heart, football is a game of territory, much like war, to which it is often compared, and which is an insult to anybody who ever fought in a war. (I once asked Dallas Cowboys defensive lineman Chad Hennings, who flew attack jets in the first Gulf War, how he felt when he heard somebody describe a game as a "battle." "I laugh," Hennings replied.)

So, with that, here's where we "kick off." With explanations about what's on the field when you're on

- offense (the guys who have the ball),
- **defense** (the guys without the ball), and
- **special teams** (the guys who kick the ball)

It's very basic stuff. *(If you know how many downs you get to advance the ball ten yards, do me a favor: skip on down.)*

First off, realize that what you can see on any TV broadcast of a game is limited by what they choose to show you. (I'm hoping that with the advent of HDTV there will someday be an option to watch the entire game from the high-angle camera that shows all twenty-two players at once. Preferably from an end-zone view. But that's in the future.)

You'll even notice a difference between network broadcasts. One network will show you a bit more of the field than the other. At least at the beginning of each play, you're pretty much limited to a tight shot of the **line of scrimmage** (the yard line on the field where the ball is placed to start a play).

The goal is to get the ball into your opponent's end zone as often as possible, however possible, and to keep him from getting the ball into your end zone. Basic, right? Let's continue.

How basic are we going to be to start?

- The offense is the side that has the ball! (Can it get more basic?) (Have you noticed that I tend to think parenthetically?)

- The offense wants to move the ball down the field—which is one hundred yards long plus a ten-yard end zone at each end—and place the ball into their opponent's end zone. That end zone is guarded by the other team's defense. When the offense moves the ball into the end zone, it's called a touchdown, which counts six points. Then, the offense can kick a ball through the upright parts of the goalpost for a single extra point (called a **PAT, or Point After Touchdown**), or run a play from the opponent's two-yard line and score a **two-point conversion.**

- Twenty-two men are on the field at a time: eleven on offense, eleven on defense. And the offense lines up (generally) like this...

| | | | X (the ball) | | | | |
|---|---|---|---|---|---|---|---|
| WR | LT | LG | C | RG | RT | TE | |
| | | | QB | | | | WR |
| | | RB | | RB | | | |

The initials stand for…

- WR Wide Receiver
- LT Left Tackle
- LG Left Guard
- C Center
- RG Right Guard
- RT Right Tackle
- TE Tight End
- QB Quarterback
- RB Running Back

Or, the way it will more likely look to you on your TV screen since teams run from left to right or vice versa…

| | | | |
|---|---|---|---|
| | | WR | |
| | | LT | |
| RB | | LG | |
| | QB | C | X (offense moves in this direction →) |
| RB | | RG | |
| | | RT | |
| | | TE | |
| | WR | | |

This is called the **T formation**, because the quarterback is right behind the center, who shoves the ball up backward between his legs to the QB to start the play. Sometimes, the QB will stand five or six yards behind the center, who'll kind of pass the ball between his legs to the QB. This is called the **shotgun formation**. Don't ask me why. I don't know everything.

The diagrams above are very basic formations. And, truth be told, you won't see these formations very often in the high-octane, spread-out offenses of today's NFL. Usually there are four receivers, or more, and one running back. The offense wants to "spread" the field, hence the name **spread formation**. They want to open up the field and make it difficult for the defense to know how they're to cover all the threats that exist at any one time.

Here's a key thing to keep in mind: no matter what the formation is, the center of the line of scrimmage will always look the same.

This is immutable. This does not change. (Well, almost never!) And in a little bit, you'll understand why it's important that you understand this.

Yes, there are hundreds of formations: some with one running back, some with no running backs, some with three receivers to one side of the offensive linemen, and many more. The only rule is you have to have seven players lined up *on* the line of scrimmage when the center snaps the ball to the quarterback.

## OFFENSE POSITIONS

To make it easier to figure out who is who on offense, they've even come up with a jersey number system:

- Centers: Numbers 50–59
- Guards & Tackles: Numbers 60–79
- Wide Receivers: Numbers 10–19 and 80–89
- Tight Ends: Numbers 80–89
- Quarterbacks: Numbers 1–19
- Running Backs: Numbers 20–49

A brief overview of each player's skills and responsibilities:

QUARTERBACK: The man

- Has the biggest salary
- Has the most responsibility
- Has to know the assignments of all eleven men on every single play
- Has to be able to "read" defenses and know what the defensive players are trying to do
- Has to have a bionic arm to throw passes on a straight line so fast that the ball wouldn't get damp if he threw it through a car wash
- Gets way too much credit for wins and way too much blame for losses
- Should never, ever date starlets

WIDE RECEIVER: Very fast, with fingers like glue

- Has the ability to cut quickly from side to side
- Has great hands to catch passes thrown at warp speed
- Can run precise routes and get to the exact same spot on the field every time, even when being hit, so that the quarterback can deliver the ball to him precisely
- Has the fearless ability to go "over the middle," where the hardest hits occur
-  Has the ability to jump up after a five-yard play, point up to the heavens, thump his chest, and proclaim himself ready for the Hall of Fame (i.e., ego)

## LEFT TACKLE: Maybe second-most important spot after the QB

- Protects the quarterback's **blind side** (Assuming the QB is right-handed, he will mostly be looking toward the right side of the field when he wants to pass, and so the defensive lineman coming from the QB's left will have a free run at him, and deck him, with the QB never knowing he was coming.)

- Built like a freight train, yet moves like a ballet dancer

- Not the best for post-game interviews, but he's not paid for his socialization skills

## LEFT GUARD: Slightly smaller than a tackle, by maybe twenty pounds, and a bit quicker

- Has to be able to fight off huge defenders while "pulling," meaning dropping off the line of scrimmage a step or two and running left or right to lead the running back to the promised land

## CENTER: The "captain" of the offensive line

- Makes calls to other linemen to let them know what kind of things the defensive line opposite them may do on the upcoming play
- Must know how to count to at least four so he snaps the ball to the QB on the right count

## RIGHT GUARD/RIGHT TACKLE: Kind of similar to the LG/LT only almost totally in reverse

- An offensive lineman once explained to me that when the coaches switched him from right tackle to left tackle, he made the switch by starting to do all his normal, daily chores left-handed: combing his hair, brushing his teeth, using his knife and fork the other way. He said this was how he convinced his brain to switch to the other side of the line, where everything is done in reverse. Kind of like the Bizzaro World in Superman!

NOTE: None of the five "interior" linemen (guards, tackles, center) are allowed to touch the ball for runs or passes, although they may recover fumbles. And every so often, you'll see a lineman come in to play what is called an **eligible receiver** position. That means he can line up where he's allowed to catch the ball. He has to report to the ref first, who announces to all the world through his microphone that "Number fifty is an eligible receiver," which should alert the defense, too. But the Patriots have a guy named Mike Vrabel who is a linebacker (a defensive position, but with a number in the fifties, so ordinarily he wouldn't be an eligible receiver). The Patriots put Vrabel in as a receiver on plays near the other team's goal line, and through 2007, he had ten catches in his career, all for touchdowns, including a couple in Super Bowl games. All of which is a long-winded way of saying that anything can, and often does, happen in the NFL.

TIGHT END: Combination blocker/receiver
- Biggest of the receivers, sometimes by fifty pounds or more
- Must be big enough to take on defensive linemen and linebackers and fast enough to run serious downfield pass routes and make big catches
- Must run precise routes, usually while being chased by large linebackers
- Must have good hands for catching of passes
- If good, can make an offense much more effective; if great, can make the Hall of Fame

RUNNING BACK: Comes in several models

- Fullback: larger, usually blocks a lot
- Halfback: smaller, faster, quicker, tougher, gets brutally hit on almost every single play
- Careers at this position are measured in dog years
- A great running back (Earl Campbell, Jim Brown, or, more contemporary, LaDanian Tomlinson) can take an offense to glory

In coach speak, the QB, RB, TE, and WR positions are called "skill positions" because they require a high degree of athleticism. The G, T, and C positions are called "strength positions" because they require the ability to lift up a Buick.

As to the aforementioned formations, there are really far too many to worry about. Just understand that if the offense has no running backs back there with the QB, and the QB is in the shotgun formation five yards behind the center, they are going to pass the ball. There is nobody there for the QB to hand off to for a run.

If they line up with three WRs to one side in a sort of tightly bunched triangle, they are going to try to confuse the defensive backs and hope one guy gets open.

### COOL THING TO SAY DURING GAME
#2

If you see the offense line up with three wide receivers to one side (kind of in a triangle), just note which side of the center they are on and then casually blurt out "Trips right" (or, "Trips left," as the case may be). It'll let everybody know you're paying attention.

# TIME-OUT #4

How tough are pro football players? It's really hard to understand. Until, and unless, you've had the chance to stand on the sidelines, you cannot understand the speed, violence, and intensity of the NFL game.

I once watched former Cowboys offensive lineman Nate Newton, all 360 pounds of him, playing table tennis. The guy moved like a ballet dancer—quick, graceful, catlike. Imagine what it must have felt like to have him get that mass going toward you for a clearing block.

During my time with the Houston Oilers, I had one experience that really drove it home for me. I was doing a post-game interview on the Oilers Radio Network with Mike Barber, a very tough tight end, who had taken quite a bit of punishment this game day. As we talked (on radio, where nobody could see us), Mike was cutting the tape off his ankles. (Football players have their ankles taped before a game for stability.) As he sliced the tape off one foot, I noticed that the sole of the foot was a brilliant purple from the heel to the place where the toes were attached. We ended the interview, and I unplugged my microphone.

"What happened to your foot?" I asked him, in a bit of disbelief.

"I tore a tendon in the bottom of it," Barber answered matter-of-factly.

"Today?"

"No. Wednesday."

"And you played today?"

"And I practiced all week."

"How could you stand it?"

"Well, they take a big ol' syringe, and they fill it up with Novocain, and they stick the needle right into the bottom of the foot. If you can take the pain of the needle, playing is easy."

"But doesn't that make your whole foot numb?"

"Up to the knee."

"How can you run?"

"Hey…they don't pay me to sit on the bench!"

I told you it was a different world.

# THE BASIC BASICS: YOUR FIRST DOWN

From whatever yard line you start off on, the rules give you four downs (plays) to go ten yards ahead. If you do that within those four plays, you get another set of four downs to gain another ten yards. Of course, if you make eighty yards in one play for a touchdown, you don't need those other three plays. There you go. That's all there is to football. You can go home now.

(Still want more, eh?) The first play of each series is called "first down" (clever, huh?), and it is the most important play of any series of downs. How you succeed on first down will determine what you can do on the next two downs. For instance, if you get six yards on first down, you then have four yards to go for another first down. So your next play, second-and-four, (second down, four yards to go for another first down) could easily be either a run or a pass, and the defense has to be on guard for anything because you could easily make that four yards by either a run or a short pass play.

But if you only gain two yards on first down, you now have second-and-eight, and it's pretty certain you'll have to pass, because getting six to eight yards on a run isn't easy. You want to get at least four to five yards consistently on first down to make headway.

There is a football statistic called "third down conversion," which means how many times you faced a third-down play and turned it into another first down. But as far as I'm concerned, if you convert every first down into another first down, you'd never face a third down and you'd be in fine shape. That's why I think first down is more important than third down. And I'm sticking to my guns on this one.

## What's our goal here?

A touchdown isn't necessarily the goal of every play. Sometimes you only want a yard or two to get a first down. Sometimes you want this play to set up the defense for the next one. Sometimes, you run a play three times in the first half so that when the same situation comes up in the second half, the defense will remember the play you ran three times in the first half and get all set to stop it, and you'll run something else entirely and fool the heck out of them. Remember, it's all a chess game.

For instance, let's say the other team punted you the ball and through no great work of your special teams (which handle **punts**, among other things), you get stuck with the ball on your own one-yard line. That's ninety-nine yards away from where you want to be, and you are in immediate danger of giving the ball back to the other team in great **field position**, meaning it'll be easy for them to score if you can't get a first down and have to punt back to them from deep in your own end zone.

So, on your own one-yard line, your first goal is to move the ball out to at least the ten-yard line, so your punter will have room to kick if he has to. Once you've advanced the ball to your own ten, you can start thinking about making yards downfield again.

So…now you understand down and distance, right? First-and-ten? Second–and-eight? Okay, let's move ahead.

(Those of you who I told to skip the basic stuff, take a peek at these next couple of paragraphs and see if you want to jump in here.)

## AT THE SNAP

When the officials set the ball on the line of scrimmage, the offense has twenty-five seconds to start a play. During that time, the quarterback will hear a play called from the coaches on the side-line into a speaker in his helmet. The quarterback's helmet has a little green sticker on it, to show that he has the speaker. Only one speaker helmet per offense is allowed on the field at a time. And the speaker is turned off when there are fifteen seconds left on the twenty-five-second clock (so the coaches can't yell in his ear, "The tight end—he's open! *The tight end!*")

The offense will set, and the defense will jump around like wild men, which many of them actually are (we'll talk about what they're doing in the chapter on defense). The offensive linemen must stay still once they take their stance. But the QB and the receivers and runners can move around a bunch, as long as they are all set for one second before the ball is snapped. One of them can actually be moving when the ball is snapped, and he's called the **man in motion**. His motion, however, can't take him *toward* the line of scrimmage.

## Vastly important item

If you've been watching football, you've probably been watching *the* football. I'm going to give you an order here:

### Don't watch the ball.

I know it sounds odd, since the ball is the whole point of the game, but the ball doesn't tell you what's going on.

The thing to watch at the moment the center snaps the ball to the QB is the offensive line, all five guys—both tackles, both guards, the center. It's really very basic. If the offensive linemen all stand straight up when the ball is snapped, it's going to be a pass. If the offensive linemen all shove forward across the line of scrimmage when the ball is snapped, it's going to be a run.

How do I know this, you ask? Simple. If the QB wants to pass, the only offensive players who can cross the line of scrimmage into the defense's territory are the eligible receivers (the

TE, WRs, and RBs). If an offensive lineman moves one yard across the line of scrimmage and a pass is thrown, that's a penalty called "ineligible man downfield." (We'll do a whole chapter about penalties and the refs later on. Be patient. Lambeau Field wasn't built in a day.)

So, line stands up straight, it's a pass. But what if they "fire out" forward? Then what you do is try to find the guards, the two linemen who flank the center. (Actually, it's probably a good idea to just watch the guards from the start.) Nine times out of ten they will lead your eye directly to what coaches call the **point of attack**, which is where the ball is going. So even though you won't see the QB hand the ball off to the running back, the guards will lead your eye to where the play is going and you'll find the running back as quickly as the defense does.

And, by watching this way, you'll be ahead of the runner—you'll see what he's going to run into, and you'll know the play's potential for success before the "fans" who haven't read this book and are therefore still watching the ball.

When you first start trying to do this, it will be very awkward. It will seem to you that everybody is running around with no particular purpose in mind, just trying to run into somebody else. But before long you will begin to see patterns emerge. Trust me. And remember, this is one of the reasons they made TiVo. Secretly tape a game, and when the Fan in your life isn't there, watch the game over, in slow motion, and go back and forth, again and again, until you begin to see the patterns in every play that I'm talking about. This is the way coaches and players look at game films. Very boring, but very instructive.

# TIME-OUT #5

Speaking of offensive linemen, a bit here about Blaine Nye, Dallas Cowboys, G, 1968–1976.

Easily the most intelligent person I ever met in the NFL. This guy was brilliant—a Stanford man, which is a heck of a start. But during his later years in the NFL, amidst the time pressures and constraints of the season, he actually earned not one but two master's degrees. Then, just after his career ended, he picked up his doctorate.

Blaine had a very low-key, laid-back sense of humor. Once, when describing the relative status of the offensive line he said, "Offensive linemen are like salt. Nobody ever remembers the brand they buy."

In a famous Cowboys comeback win on Thanksgiving Day, 1974, QB Roger Staubach was knocked out, and the somewhat clueless and very offbeat backup Clint Longley came in to throw key TD passes for the victory over the hated Redskins.

In the locker room, a reporter asked Nye what the game meant. He looked over at Longley and said, "This game represents the triumph of the uncluttered mind."

Nye and his fellow low-key teammates Larry Cole and Pat Toomay formed what they called "The Zero Club," which was dedicated to the art of doing as little as possible. About the most initiative they ever really took was the time Toomay and Nye threatened to take blond, Nordic-looking Larry Cole and have a tattoo placed on his upper arm reading

"Born to Raise Wheat."

Nye once explained to me, during an NFL labor dispute, how the league was not a monopoly, but actually a "bilateral oligopoly." Well, he told it to me, really. I can't call it an explanation, because I still don't understand a thing he said. But he was, and remains, my all-time favorite interview.

I was interviewing him after one game and noticed his right index finger was swollen and ugly purple and about the size of a Polish sausage.

"When did that happen?" I asked Nye.

"First quarter," he said quietly.

"Didn't it hurt?"

"You don't think about it during the game."

"When do you think about it?"

A tear rolled down from his eye.

"Now."

## TWO GREAT WAYS TO RUN THE BALL

A great running back can be the most exciting of athletes. With incredible peripheral vision, strength, speed, quickness, and guts, the running back is the workhorse of the offense. If he carries the ball, he gets hit hard. If they fake a handoff to him, he gets hit hard. If he blocks, he gets to hit, but he still gets hit. It's a brutal position.

In my on-air career, I had the weekly chance to watch two of the best: Earl Campbell of the Houston Oilers and Emmitt Smith of the Dallas Cowboys. Totally different runners, totally different builds, totally different styles. But both are at the top of the RB food chain.

One amazing play from each...

### Earl

1978: Earl's rookie year with Houston, and each week our jaws drop more and more often as we watch what this guy with the thirty-four-inch thighs (each) can do. The Oilers were hosting the L.A. Rams in the Astrodome, and the Rams had a big linebacker (for those times) named Isaiah Robertson.

Well, Earl got the handoff and headed up the middle, and Robertson came up toward him looming like Dracula about to bite, his arms held high and wide over his head. He was going to just drape himself all over the upstart rookie Campbell and crush him.

Earl lowered his head and buried his helmet between the five and the eight on Robertson's jersey and simply bowled him backward about three yards. Earl gained another twenty yards before the Rams could stop him.

Years after this play, I met Robertson at a charity golf tournament.

"Should I tell you that I was one of the Oilers radio announcers in 1978?" I jokingly asked him.

His eyes narrowed into an intense stare.

"No!"

## Emmitt

1995: Cowboys are hosting Denver at Texas Stadium. Early in the game, the Cowboys are on about the Denver thirty, and QB Troy Aikman calls a pass play. Emmitt Smith stays in and lays a crushing block on a charging Denver linebacker, flattening the guy.

"Whoa," I say to myself, "impressive block."

But it ain't over. Emmitt gets up, runs out into Denver territory, and Troy throws a ten-yard pass to him for a first down.

That's the kind of complete player Emmitt was. You don't wind up as the all-time NFL rushing yardage leader without both talent and smarts.

What was the main difference between Emmitt and Earl? Supporting cast. Emmitt has three Super Bowl rings, Earl has none. Had the two switched teams, they still both would have been great, and Earl would have had the jewelry.

## THE RUNNING GAME

Whether or not you believe the coach cliché that "you run to set up the pass" doesn't matter. You have to have both to win. A good running game does three things:

- it keeps the defense honest, forcing them to worry about both the run and the pass;
- it moves the ball down the field; and
- it eats up the clock, because unless you run out of bounds, the clock keeps on ticking. That's why you see teams run the ball

so much if they are ahead in the fourth quarter.

Of course, the guys carrying the ball wouldn't be much good without the guys up front **blocking** for them. And blocking for runs usually takes two forms. (Remember: you're going to be looking for the guards at the snap of the ball, right?) The two types of blocking are called **man** and **zone**, and those terms will also come up later in pass defense. But on the offensive side of the ball, they mean the following.

## "Man" blocking

It's kind of just what it sounds like: "man" blocking, meaning this "man" blocks one other "man." The actual term would be "man on man," but we speak shorthand in football. So if you see each of the linemen taking on one guy in a sort of haphazard, Keystone Kops fashion, it's probably man blocking. In that case, the running back is supposed to go right toward a specific space between two blockers. This space is called the **hole**, and it's that hole that the running back wants to sprint through to get past the linemen and into the secondary, where the smaller defensive backs are. So generally, on plays like this, the running back will take the handoff and make a beeline for the hole. Holes are almost vaporous and tend to close up quicker than a bar in Baptist country. You gotta hit 'em quick.

## "Zone" blocking

"Zone" blocking is again kind of self-explanatory. The linemen just shove their way through a particular zone on the field, kind of sweeping away everything before them like a bulldozer. Oftentimes, when they are zone blocking, the line will look like the Rockettes. Not that they'll kick really high, but they'll all move the same way, off the same foot, in the same direction, at the snap of the ball. When the five linemen move as a unit in one direction, it's zone blocking.

> ### COOL THING TO SAY DURING GAME
> #### #3
>
> The first time you actually recognize zone blocking, say softly to yourself but loud enough for others in the room to hear, "Nice zone blocking scheme." They will really think you know your stuff. If they ask you to elaborate, tell them, "Just watch. You'll pick it up."

Simply put, the offensive linemen are trying to push the defensive linemen where they don't want to go, to get them out of the running back's way. The defensive linemen want to stay right where they are, and clog up the hole to keep the running back from getting through.

## Typecasting

Remember earlier we talked about Emmitt Smith and Earl Campbell? The quick, darting little guy and the big, bruising crusher? Those are pretty much the two basic types of running back, and a good team will have one of each. They won't both be Hall-of-Fame caliber, but they'll complement each other.

The Cowboys recently had an interesting setup with Julius Jones, the darter, and Marion Barber, the crusher. For several seasons they used the two in tandem. Jones would start, and would occasionally rack up some good numbers. Barber would come in late in the first and, especially, second half, when the defense was getting tired, and would pound them again and again. Fans wondered why Barber wasn't getting to start, as his yards-per-carry stat (the gold standard for running backs) was usually always better than Jones could manage. For the 2007 regular season, Barber averaged 4.8 yards per carry, which is a superb number (anything over 4 and people take notice). Jones, the starter, averaged 3.6...workman-like, but no big deal.

In their divisional playoff game against the Giants in 2007, they made the switch, starting Barber, and it turned out to be a huge mistake. Barber stayed at 4.8 and had a pretty good game with 129 yards on 27 carries. But 101 of those yards came in the first half, and the clock-killing presence he brought to the second half was no longer there. Jones fell to only 2.7 yards per carry and added nothing as the Cowboys lost to the eventual Super Bowl champs. It's a delicate balance, and just because one of your running backs is a bruiser and one is a smaller, quicker guy, they may not always make a great tandem. It's a "chemistry" thing.

## THE PASSING GAME

Okay, it's glamour time. Let's talk about quarterbacks and receivers and lightning strikes down the field and changing the course of the game in one play. It's in the passing game where watching on TV really restricts you. When you don't get to see all twenty-two players at once, you don't get a sense of how deep the safeties (the last line of defense) are playing. You can't often tell how the cornerbacks (who cover the speedy wide receivers), are shading their man. Since the TV director doesn't know when a pass is coming, he can't widen out the shot, so you're still stuck watching the line.

But again, if you've been paying attention, you know what to look for. Fill in the blank:

*When the offensive line _____ at the snap of the ball, it's a pass.*

(If you answered "stands up," take an extra hot dog.)

And of course, if you're still watching the QB and he drops back with the ball in his hand and he's looking downfield, you can pretty much look for a pass as well.

The legendary University of Texas coach Darrell Royal used to say that three things could happen when you pass, and two of them are bad: completion, good; incompletion, bad; **interception**, worse. He could have added **sack** or fumble or who knows what all to his list. But in today's NFL, the passing game sells tickets. When Brett Favre announced his retirement (though he later un-retired, depending on what's going on with him when you read this), people weren't sad to see him go because they enjoyed spelling his name. They were going to miss his gambler's attitude, his amazing arm, and the way he rallied his team, and the city of Green Bay, on game day.

So, what do you want to do when you pass?

- Strike downfield quickly

- Pick up quick first downs

- Keep the defense "honest" by backing them off the line of scrimmage, opening up the run

- Score touchdowns! (Doh!)

What's the toughest pass for an NFL QB, or any other QB for that matter, to throw consistently well?

No, it's not the bomb, the seventy-yard downfield killer. It's the one called the "sideline" route, where the receiver will go about five yards downfield and then cut toward the nearest sideline. Here's why it's the toughest pass: The quarterback may only have to throw the ball about five yards downfield, but if you picture the geometry of the field in your mind, you'll realize he's throwing down the hypotenuse of a right triangle. So even if the receiver is "only" five yards downfield, the pass can take up to forty yards (depending on the distance from the sideline). This makes it easy for the defender to intercept the pass because he has very little ground to make up to get to the man he's covering before the ball arrives, which makes for an easier "pick" (football talk for "interception").

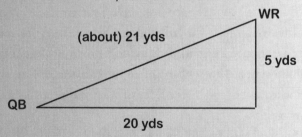

QB only throws ball 5 yards downfield, but about 21 yards in the air, giving the defensive back lots of time to come up and make interception. Put the QB farther from the sideline, and the distance gets even tougher.

# TIME-OUT #6

It's 1977 in Thousand Oaks, California, and I'm covering my first Dallas Cowboys training camp. Very heady stuff for a twenty-five-year-old sportscaster.

Anyway, during the annual Blue-White scrimmage, the first time in camp the offense and defense really mix it up, a bunch of us media types are standing on the sidelines watching. Roger Staubach is running the first team offense and his backup, Danny White, is getting ready to come in.

Well, not quite getting ready. He calls out, "Mark!" I turn around.

"Can you catch a couple quick so I can warm up?" He makes a throwing motion with the ball in his hand.

"Sure," I say, displaying a bravado wholly unsuited to my actual football ability.

Danny is about twenty-five yards away from me, and he lets fly. I can hear the ball coming before it gets to me. It smacks into my extended palms and drives my hands back into my chest. I barely hang on to the ball, some of the wind knocked out of me by the force of what was probably a very average pass.

Feebly, I toss the ball back to Danny.

"Let me find you somebody who gets paid to do this," I tell him.

Those guys throw very, very hard.

## Receivers

As mentioned earlier, you can break receivers down into two basic types: wide receivers and tight ends. Running backs also get in on the action, but even when they catch passes, they're still running backs. Receivers are designed almost exclusively to get downfield and catch the ball.

The receivers generally each have a specific set of pass routes they run (the specifically outlined way a receiver gets from point A to point B, where the QB then throws him the ball), and every receiver is better at some routes than at others. There are short routes designed to hit quickly and move the ball steadily downfield. There are deep routes designed to take advantage of a size or speed differential between the receiver and the defensive back assigned to guard him. (And at the pro level, the receiver better run his route to the same, exact spot downfield every single time, because the QB is going to throw it right to that spot every single time. The precision is really something.)

As the offense lines up, check to see if the defender opposite the WR is playing tight (right up on the line) or loose (back five or more yards). This can give you a hint of what the defense expects. If the defender is tight, he'll try to "jam" the receiver at the line of scrimmage and throw him off stride.

Look to see if the tight end is lined up right next to one of the offensive tackles, or if he's split out a ways. The further out from the tackle the tight end is, the more likely a pass play is coming up.

And you can always tell who the toughest receivers are because they're the ones who run routes right across the middle—"crossing" routes, where the receiver goes five yards out and then cuts parallel to the line of scrimmage. Or the "slant," where the receiver takes a forty-five-degree angle upfield. On those passes there is almost always a defensive back coming at the receiver at top speed, trying to get there the same instant the ball does. The collisions are frightening. The great ones learn how to let their bodies go almost limp, to absorb the punishment.

My old friend and broadcast colleague Drew Pearson was an ace at these plays. In fact, he used to call the middle of the field "Drew's space." And, if you happen to be one of those sportswriters who votes for the Pro Football Hall of Fame, Drew deserves to be in there!

## Quarterbacks

Obviously if you're talking pass, you're talking quarterback. It's what they get paid for. It's what moves the ball down the field. It's what the fans love to see. Just as the QB must understand every offensive lineman's assignment on every play, he must also know every receiver's route on every play. On top of that, he must know the habits and tendencies of the defense he's trying to pass the ball into. He has to have something approaching a computer of a mind to be able to gaze up and down and all across the field in about two seconds and estimate which receiver has the best chance of being open.

*COOL THING TO SAY DURING GAME*
*#5*

If you see the QB shifting his head from side to side as he drops back, kick back in your recliner and say, "He really sees the whole field." Jaws will drop.

In today's NFL, the basic play is called into the QB via his helmet radio, and he must add to the call the formation that makes the most sense given the players he has on the field. As the team approaches the line of scrimmage, his eyes are already scanning the defense, checking out who is where, and trying to determine what will happen at the snap of the ball. If he sees lots of things he doesn't like (meaning if the defense is somehow in great position to foil the particular play called), he'll scream a lot of stuff out loud. If one of the code words he calls is the key, that means the next stuff he says is going to change the play right at the line. This is called an **audible**.

You'll oftentimes see a receiver go in motion before the snap. (Remember, one man can be moving parallel to the line of scrimmage before and at the snap of the ball.) Sometimes this is done to actually change the formation. Sometimes it's done to let the QB and the receivers see if the defense is playing "man for man" (one defensive back on one receiver) or "zone" (each defender covering a specific area on the field.) (And do we remember those "man" and "zone" terms from our discussion of blocking schemes?) If the motion receiver crosses from one end of the line of scrimmage to the other, and one defensive back shadows him the entire time, it's probably man-to-man coverage, and everybody adjusts accordingly.

> ### COOL THING TO SAY DURING GAME
> #### #6
>
> As an addendum to letting everybody know that you think the QB sees the whole field, if he drops back to pass and looks like he's trying to keep his feet off burning coals and wastes time and doesn't find a receiver, announce to the room that, "This guy's got happy feet."

When the ball is snapped, the QB drops backward, all the while keeping his eyes on what's going on downfield. His eyes will dart back and forth and up and down the field in a progression of "reads" as he searches for the receiver who has the best shot at being open enough to throw to.

All the while that he's scanning the field, at least three, and usually more, huge people are running toward him, fighting off blockers, making all sorts of ungodly noise and wishing only to place the QB firmly on his backside. (Called a "sack" if they tackle him while he still has the ball. Called a "pressure" if it's just after he's let the ball go. Called "roughing the passer" and penalized if it's too long after he's let the pass go.)

Just as the gutsy receivers are the ones who go over the middle, the gutsy QBs are the ones who stand in the **pocket** no matter how intense the pressure. Keep your eye on the QB's feet. (I know, I'm telling you to watch a whole bunch of different stuff, aren't I? Switch around from play to play. Learn the whole game. See the whole field!) If he stands almost rock steady, barely shifting his weight around as he looks for the open man, he's doing fine. If he kind of dances around, turning this way and that, he's said to have "happy feet," and that's not a happy thing to have. It means that when the moment comes to throw, his feet may not be set completely, his weight may be awkwardly distributed, and the pass won't be as exact as it should be. Remember: god is in the details.

## PLAY-ACTION PASS

**Play-action** is where the run and the pass combine, where you use one to set up the other all in one play.

In a play-action pass, the first thing that happens is the QB fakes a handoff to his running back. Now, since you'll be watching the offensive line, you may miss this (until your field of vision increases, which it will, and you start seeing the whole screen at once). The running back will head into the line bent over, crouching like he has the ball, and he'll get popped by the defensive line. The QB will drop back bent over, as if he actually handed the ball off. But he didn't. He's still got it. (The Colts' Peyton Manning does this as well as anybody ever.) And he'll stand up and pop it off quickly, hoping that the run fake has "frozen" the linebackers and defensive backs (hoping they stop dropping back and come forward to meet the run). If they have been frozen, even for half a second, that can be all the time the passing game needs to succeed.

The receiver can fly downfield, the QB launches the pass, and it's TD dance time in the end zone.

## THE RED ZONE

When you get close to the other team's end zone, which is where you want to be, you're in what is called the red zone, inside the other team's twenty-yard line. Things change in the red zone. They get a lot more difficult for several reasons:

- The other guy doesn't want you in his end zone. You're after his family, his money, his honor. He's going to be upset with you.

- As you now have only twenty yards of field plus ten yards of end zone to work with, that means you only have thirty yards of field in which to run pass routes. Which means that you can't run really deep routes, and the defensive backs have less area to cover so they can be more aggressive.

- As you can't throw the ball deep now, you also can't "put a lot of air under it." You have to throw your passes with a lot more zip, on a flatter trajectory, so they get to the receiver in a hurry.

The main thing you want to do in any red zone visit is come away with points. When you get down that close, you want at least a **field goal**, if not a TD. Red zone success is one of the stats to keep a close eye on. The offense will have specially designed plays to use only in the red zone.

**COOL THING TO SAY DURING GAME**
**#7**

When your team fails to score in the red zone, shake your head slowly from side to side and say, "That's why coaches get prematurely gray."

# TIME-OUT #7

How good are the great ones?

Well, you can see Tom Brady or Peyton Manning do their stuff on the field all the time. But that's just the easy stuff.

In the Cowboys locker room one day, offensive lineman Mark Tuinei stood at the opposite end of the room from QB Troy Aikman. Now, the Cowboys locker room at their practice facility is quite large, so Tuinei was likely forty-five feet or so away from his teammate.

Aikman was tossing a football back and forth in his hands as he talked to somebody. Tuinei had just finished a can of soda. He looked across the room and yelled, "Hey, eight-ball!" (Aikman's jersey number was eight. His nickname was "eight-ball." That's about as creative as nicknames get anymore.)

Aikman turned to him. Tuinei put the soda can on top of his head.

"Go ahead. Knock it off."

Aikman, never one to refuse a William Tell challenge like this said, "Do you want me to throw it hard or soft?"

"Soft," Tuinei said, "just in case."

Aikman looked, pumped, and lofted the ball across the room, where it lightly brushed the can from the top of Tuinei's head. And Mark never flinched.

Tuinei, sad to say, eventually died of an overdose. A great loss to the game.

## Two-minute drill

You've surely noticed that when there are two minutes left in either half, the ref blows the whistle and announces the "two-minute warning." This serves two purposes. First, it allows the networks to take another commercial break and pay the bills. Second, it assures both benches that even if they don't have anybody smart enough to read the time left on the clock, they'll at least know when there are two minutes remaining.

In this two-minute time period, teams will run what they call the **two-minute drill**. This is an area of the game designed to eat up the most real estate possible while eating up as little of the clock as possible.

Teams will call two plays in the huddle and run them back-to-back, without a huddle, to put pressure on the defense. Or they'll simply go to their "no huddle," offense, where the QB will call plays at the line of scrimmage so the defense can't make any substitutions of players. (Teams spend quite a bit of practice time in training camp and during the season on the two-minute offense.)

Often, fans will be concerned when their team's defense calls time-out in the last two minutes of a half, wondering why they don't leave those time-outs for the offense to use. The simple reason is that defensive time-outs save more time than offensive ones. Since the offense can stop the clock intentionally by throwing the ball out of bounds, running it out of bounds, or running the **clock play**, where the QB intentionally throws the ball into the ground at his feet to stop the clock, the offense can control time quite handily. The defense can't. So by calling defensive time-outs, your defense is actually preserving game time for your offense to get the ball back and do something with it. Defensive time-outs save an average of forty-five seconds.

As they move down the field, the offense will try to position the ball where they need it. If they only need a field goal to tie or win, the offense wants to make it easy for their kicker, so they'll try to keep the ball in the center of the field, between the **hash marks** (a series of marks on the field, the width of the goalposts, at each yard line). If the play ends between the hash marks, the ball is placed down where it is. If the play ends with the ball outside the hash, the ball is moved to the nearest hash for the next play. If the offense is driving for a touchdown, the hash marks don't really matter, only the end zone does.

---

### COOL THING TO SAY DURING GAME
#### #8

If you're watching a game and one of your friends chastises the coach for calling defensive time-outs near the end of a half, say, very patiently, like a teacher to a young schoolboy who hasn't quite mastered "i before e" yet, "Defensive time-outs save more time than offensive time-outs!"

---

Nothing irritates me more, as a broadcaster or a fan, than to see a team fail to try to score when they have the ball late in the first half. Late in a half, coaches will sometimes tell their QB to simply kneel down, and the ref will blow the play dead. This is a way of telling the other team you're not going to run a play where any injury might occur. It's sort of the football equivalent of a white flag. However, toward the end of a game, when you kneel down, you're saying you know you've won and you won't try to score anymore. When Barry Switzer was coaching the Cowboys, he had Troy Aikman take a knee toward the end of a game against Green Bay. Then, somebody told Switzer that kicker Chris Boniol was only one field goal away from setting a new team record for most field goals in a game. Switzer started running plays again to get in field goal distance and then let Boniol kick the record-breaker. I thought that running yardage-gaining plays again after taking the knee was an amateurish move on Switzer's part then, and I said so on the air after the game, and I still think so today.

But, back to our story. Running one play where the QB kneels down is okay if there's only a second left, but if you get the ball with forty-five seconds to play, try to score. That's what the game is about.

> **COOL THING TO SAY DURING GAME**
> **#9**
>
> To really make the point, when the two-minute time-out commercial break is over, as your team comes up to the line of scrimmage and your QB goes under center, swirl your drink, make that ice noise, and say, "Work the sideline, baby!"

Players have made their reputations on the two-minute warning—Roger Staubach, the Cowboys' legendary QB of the seventies, and Tom Brady of the current Patriots, to name a couple. Simply put, winning teams know how to handle the two-minute period. So don't you use that time-out as an excuse to refresh the chips and dip; get ready for action. Suggest the first two plays your team should run. Or, if your defense is on the field, tell them what to watch out for. This will impress mightily the people watching the game with you. They'll think you must have read a book or something.

## HOT RECEIVERS

No, it's not about players who are incredibly good looking. The "hot" receiver is the receiver who has gone into an area vacated by a blitzing defender.

Now, I know we're getting a bit ahead into defense here, but hang with me. Ordinarily, the defense just sends in three or four linemen to try to sack the quarterback. But they will also send linebackers or defensive backs on **blitz** plays (another of those war terms).

If it's a blitz the quarterback sees before him (as opposed to one behind him, on his blind side, that he can't see), he first looks into the area that the blitzing player vacated to charge at him. If it's a linebacker, it'll be a certain area; if it's a safety, it'll be a different area. If his receivers do their job, one of them will have slipped into that vacated area and be the recipient of a very quick pass designed to fill that gap, gain some quick yardage, and save the quarterback from being knocked on his you-know-what. And it all has to happen in about one-fifth the time it took you to read this paragraph.

## OFFENSE INSTANT REPLAY

- There are four downs to get ten yards for another set of four downs
- First down is key; gain four or more yards on first down to be effective
- They can run the ball, or they can pass it
- WATCH THE LINEMEN, NOT THE BALL! The linemen show you where the play is going
- Red zone: inside the defense's twenty-yard line
- Two-minute drill: defensive time-outs save time for the offense

# HALFTIME: THE TEN MOST IMPORTANT FIGURES IN NFL HISTORY

# HALFTIME: THE TEN MOST IMPORTANT FIGURES IN NFL HISTORY

R efresh everybody's drink and snacks. See if the pizza has arrived. Read the following list.

My Own List (therefore official)

## 10. GEORGE PLIMPTON

Got you from the start! The sophisticated New York author spent a training camp with the Detroit Lions in the sixties, played QB for one series in practice, and wrote one of the greatest sports books of all time: *PAPER LION*. He helped humanize the game for millions.

## 9. THE GUY WHO INVENTED INSTANT REPLAY

Probably many guys. Instant replay was actually first used on an Army-Navy telecast in 1963, (Roger Staubach QB for Navy), and it changed viewing TV forever. And when they began to slow replays down, it changed even more. The subtleties of the game could now be made apparent to the casual viewer. We all got smarter. Pretty soon, we all knew as much as Vince Lombardi (the great Packers coach of the fifties and sixties after whom the Super Bowl trophy is named).

## 8. ED SABOL (and, by extension, John Facenda)

In 1960, Ed Sabol bid for the rights to film the NFL championship game—for three grand. From this start, an empire was born, called NFL Films—the greatest propaganda use of film since Leni Riefenstahl. At some point in your life, whether you know it or not, you've watched something from NFL Films. They have slowed the game down to give it a ballet-like grace, and made the violence almost poetic. Their music, their words, everything they do is brilliant. And, speaking of words, you have to note the late, great John Facenda, the quintessential NFL Films voice. Even though it's doubtful he ever said Lambeau Field was a "frozen tundra," as is so famously attributed, just hearing his voice means football for millions.

## 7. JOE NAMATH

He guaranteed a Super Bowl III New York Jets win over the Baltimore Colts, then made it come true. He gave the American Football League legitimacy, star power, and excitement. He *was* the sixties as far as pro football went. Without his Super Bowl win, the merger of the NFL and AFL might have taken much longer to achieve parity, at least in the minds of the fans. He made the two leagues equal in sixty minutes.

## 6. RED GRANGE

When the "Galloping Ghost" came out of the University of Illinois in 1924, college football was everything. Pro football was for illiterate mill workers to bash each other to bits for two bucks a game. Then Grange signed with George Halas for the Chicago Bears, and all of a sudden, pro football games were played in huge stadia rather than on sandlots. The $70,000 he earned in 1924 equals well over a million in today's dough. Along with baseball's Babe Ruth and golfer Bobby Jones, he was at the pinnacle of the golden sports era of the 1920s.

I met Grange at Super Bowl XII, when he was the honorary tosser of the coin. He was old, but still upright, fit, and full of fascinating stories.

## 5. BYRON DONZIS

Got you again, didn't I?

Going into a game against the New Orleans Saints in 1978, Houston Oilers quarterback Dan Pastorini's ribs were so cracked and broken that he had to have Novocain injections in between each of his ribs on each side of his chest, before the game and again at the half. On returning to Houston, he checked into a hospital for treatment before the next week's first-round playoff game.

As he lay in his bed in a painkiller-induced stupor, he looked up to see a grizzly man at his bedside, wearing a trench coat and holding a baseball bat.

"Oh, god," Pastorini thought. "Somebody lost money on the game and they're gonna kill me."

Instead, the man handed the baseball bat to his assistant and said, "Watch."

The assistant swung as hard as he could, hitting the man squarely in the ribs. The man didn't even flinch. He opened his trench coat and showed Pastorini what was the prototype for the quarterback "flak jacket," now standard football issue. "I want one of those!" Pastorini said.

He wore it the next week, and Byron Donzis, the man in the trench coat, went on to become one of the most important inventors in NFL history.

## 4. ROONE ARLEDGE

The visionary head of ABC Sports who came up with the idea of putting an NFL game on ABC at a time when the network was dying. It was Monday night, 9:00 p.m. (EST). The country's viewing habits, and more, changed. Movie theaters and restaurants were empty on Monday evenings. Everybody watched. Everybody quoted Howard Cosell the next day. Sport grew up and prime time became play time. You could easily argue that Roone should be number one. You could also make your own list.

## 3. TEX SCHRAMM & LAMAR HUNT

Tex Schramm, the Cowboys' first president and general manager, and Lamar Hunt, the original owner of the Kansas City Chiefs, were the architects of the 1970 NFL-AFL merger. The two leagues were spending each other out of existence, and the war of attrition looked to be endless. Schramm and Hunt held a series of secret meetings and smoothed things out so that the two leagues could become one. Many testy items had to be ironed out, including the moving of three teams—the Colts, Browns, and Steelers—from the NFL to the AFL (renamed the AFC), so that each conference under the new, unified league would have the same number of franchises. So, in today's NFL, there are two conferences, the American and the National, and each conference has some teams from the old AFL and some from the old NFL.

These two men were influential far beyond the merger. It was Hunt who came up with the name "Super Bowl" among many other innovations. And he was one of the nicest, most genuine people you could ever hope to meet.

Tex was a large, lively, blustery man who loved nothing more than a good argument.

My first road trip with the Cowboys, as a twenty-five-year-old sportscaster, was in 1977, to Minnesota and the old Vikings stadium, the Met.

The Cowboys had the Vikings on their own one-yard line. Viking QB Fran Tarkenton dropped back into his own end zone and, finding no receivers, threw the ball into the ground. The ref threw a flag for intentional grounding, the penalty called when the quarterback throws a pass intended to be incomplete to avoid his being sacked for a loss of yardage.

I was seated next to Tex in the press box as the ref marked off half the distance to the goal line, the correct penalty at the time. Tex slammed his fist on the counter and said, "#$#%#, next year, that's gonna be a **safety**!"

Tex was the head of the NFL Competition Committee, the group that sets the rules.

Next year…intentional grounding in your own end zone became a safety! And it still is today.

## 2. GEORGE HALAS

One of the NFL's founders, owner of the franchise originally known as the Decatur Staleys, but eventually the Chicago Bears. Halas was an NFL owner/coach/legend for over sixty years. "Papa Bear" took the league from its literal beginnings as a group of ragtag men playing in rock-strewn fields adjacent to coal mines, to the heights of Monday Night Football and Super Bowls.

When he offered what his all-pro tight end Mike Ditka thought was a too-small contract, Ditka said, "Halas tosses nickels around like they were manhole covers."

## 1. PETE ROZELLE

Commissioner from 1960 to 1990. It was Rozelle, a former PR guy for the L.A. Rams, who not only oversaw the many egos of the owners through the merger, but got them to see that Roone Arledge had a good idea, etc. His key contribution came when Rozelle convinced the owners that the only way the NFL would survive in every size market was to take all that lovely TV money and share it equally. Revenue sharing, along with the player draft and much more, is what keeps the NFL on a competitive footing, from New York to Green Bay. Everybody who wants to study the sport and how it works has to study Rozelle.

Not to mention that he was his own league's best PR man. He knew the name of every beat reporter and sportscaster around the league and was always willing to sit for interviews and spread some inside info.

Absent Pete Rozelle, the NFL would have remained a nice little sports group for the few, not the amazing monolith it is today.

# DEFENSE: CHASE 'EM AND CATCH 'EM

# DEFENSE: CHASE 'EM AND CATCH 'EM

When I was with the Houston Oilers' radio crew from 1978–81, the Oilers had a defensive back named Willie Alexander who was one of the more thoughtful athletes I ever met: soft-spoken, dignified, and very insightful about the game he played. I once asked him what the difference was between offense and defense.

COOL THING TO SAY DURING GAME
#10

When your defense is on the field, just call them, "The D." If you must use the full word, it's pronounced DEE-fense, like you're from the south. If somebody calls them the "de-FENSE," tell them that "De-FENSE is the thing that goes around de-YARD."

"The offense are the artists—the great creators. They paint these lovely pictures, these complex portraits," Willie said.

"We (the defense) are the destroyers. We love to come in and lay waste to what they have made. We deconstruct. We storm the museum and trash all the lovely paintings."

That's about as good a definition of defensive football as I've ever come across.

While your offense is trying to put the ball across the goal line, their defense is doing everything they can to stop you. They are delivering the harsh blows, creating mass confusion, bringing havoc to all parts of the field. And they do it with men who range from slight (I used to tell Willie he was an inspiration to people with skinny legs) to huge (remember "Refrigerator" Perry? He'd just be average sized today).

No slam against offense, but most of the really analytical, complex thinkers I've known in football have been on defense. Charlie Waters, the great Dallas Cowboys safety of the 1970s, put more thought into defense than anybody I ever knew. Part of that was an effort to improve his chances as his physical talent may not have been on a par with everybody else. But part of it was simply his innate curiosity and intellect at play.

Charlie once spent half an hour breaking down for me the intricacies of blocking a punt. Now most of us would think, "Run toward the punter, jump, stick out arms, block kick." But there was a ton more: angles, tendencies, game situations, field position. Charlie is just intense!

## THE BASICS FOR THE "D"

As with offense, the defense lines up in many different ways, depending on the situation, the personnel called for, etc. But basically, here's the "D."

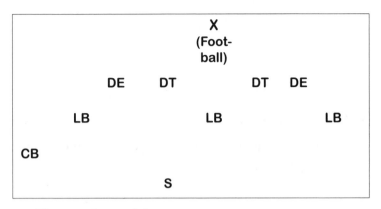

The initials stand for…

- DE Defensive End
- DT Defensive Tackle
- LB Linebacker
- CB Cornerback
- S Safety

As with the offense, the above diagram is very basic. This is the 4-3, meaning four linemen on the line of scrimmage and three linebackers behind them. Most defenses are named for the number of linemen and linebackers. Often you'll see teams in a 3-4, which is simply three linemen and four linebackers. You'll also hear a lot about "**nickel**" packages. If the announcers talk about a team going to the "nickel," that simply means they've taken out somebody (usually a linebacker) and put in an extra defensive back. So instead of the usual four defensive backs, there are now five. Get it—five! Nickel! (I never said all this stuff was clever.)

## DEFENSIVE POSITIONS

As with offense, the defensive players' jerseys are number-coded as well.

- Defensive Linemen wear 60–79

- Linebackers wear 50–59
- Cornerbacks and Safeties wear 20–49

## DEFENSIVE END: Fast and furious

- Must be both very strong and very quick
- Responsible for putting heated, ugly, yelling, spitting pressure on the QB as well as making sure that running plays don't get outside them to break off big gains down the sideline
- They learn to do lots of martial arts stuff with their hands and arms to ward off offensive linemen
- The best end is usually the one on the defensive right side. He's the one who rushes the QB from the blind side. (The one whom, you'll recall, the offensive left tackle has to handle. So the best "matchup" is usually between left offensive tackle and right defensive end.)

## DEFENSIVE TACKLE: Big and ornery

- Must be even stronger than the defensive end
- Will generally run into double-team blocking, where two offensive linemen will take him on at once
- As he fights off two 300-pound-plus blockers he must keep his head up, "read" the play (figure out what the offense is doing), and move toward the ball
- Oftentimes his job is to sacrifice his body by clogging up the lanes in the middle and making life annoying for the running back
- On running plays, you'll likely see a tackle engaging his opposing lineman and then moving laterally along the line of scrimmage, trying to jam up the holes and give the ball carrier no place to run. He's got to move laterally, though. If he gets

pushed backward, the runner will get positive yardage. It's all about protecting your turf

## LINEBACKER: Hybrids of defense

- A cross between the line and the defensive backs.

- Must be physically strong and tough enough to take on blockers and stop the running game, while also quick and agile enough to get into pass coverage and stay with receivers.

- The LB who plays on the same side of the field as the offense's tight end is known as the "strong-side" linebacker, because the tight end provides one extra blocker to that side. The strong-side LB is generally a little bit bigger and, yes, stronger.

- The linebacker on the side without the tight end is called the "weak-side" linebacker. But there's really nothing weak about him. He just gets more open field action.

## CORNERBACK: Living on the edge

- Probably the best athlete on defense.

- CBs have to be very quick and very fast, the difference being that *quick* is how instantaneously you get up to speed, and *fast* is how much speed you get up to.

- They have to have high self-esteem, because they are often going one-on-one way out there in the open with great receivers. (See elsewhere for Gene Stallings' speech to young cornerbacks to find out the dangers of the job.) When a corner makes a mistake, everybody in the stands knows it, and everybody watching at home knows it because they run the replay again and again and again.

- The best corners are called "shutdown" corners, because they shut a receiver down and totally "take away that side of the field" from the passing game.

- They are often outgoing, gregarious types who love danger, both on and off the field.

## SAFETIES: The last line of defense

- The guys who line up farthest downfield; if the play gets by them, it's all over, and the offense kicks a PAT.

- Usually bigger and more violent than the corners.

- They have to "come up" and offer run support, meaning if it's a running play they dash forward and help the linebackers make the stop. Some of the bigger safeties will actually play up front in the linebacker's area.

- Occasionally, they do things that are less than kosher, and have rules named after them. Cowboys safety Roy Williams was notorious for grabbing the back of a player's shoulder pads, just under his helmet, and "horse-collaring" him to the ground. Many who were tackled this way broke bones and suffered other injuries. A horse-collar tackle is now illegal in the NFL, and the rule is generally called the "Roy Williams rule," an honor he'd probably be happier without. (Williams also admitted, on a radio talk show, that there were times when he hoped the QB wouldn't throw the ball to the man he was covering. An amazing admission because, (1) all great athletes want the action to come their way and (2) QBs and coaches all over the NFL will now scout Cowboys game films to find the situations Williams is uncomfortable in, and throw that stuff at him twice as often.)

Just as the offense is a very interdependent machine, the defense relies on the sum of its parts, too. The better pass rush you get from your defensive line, the less pressure the linebackers and defensive backs will feel from the pass. The stronger and quicker your linebackers, the more chances you can take with exotic pass coverages and blitzes. The better your defensive backs can cover, the harder it is for receivers to get open, giving the defensive line more time to rush the quarterback, which creates less pressure for the linebackers and defensive backs, etc.

### COOL THING TO SAY DURING GAME
### #11

This one's almost too easy, as you are a much more skilled critic of the game at this point. But if a tackler does drag somebody down by the back of the neck, and the refs mark off the penalty for a "horse-collar," exhale softly and say, "Ah, yes…the Roy Williams rule."

# TIME-OUT #8

Speaking of Charlie Waters, which I was, a few pages back, Charlie was one of the best safeties of his era (1970–81). But there was a brief time when the Cowboys put him at cornerback, a position he was wholly unsuited to play as it requires keeping up with the fastest of receivers.

One of his few games at the position was a Monday-nighter in Washington against the hated Redskins and their Hall of Fame receiver, Charley Taylor. And Taylor had a field day. (Or would it be "field night"?) He caught a couple of touchdowns against Waters, and after the last one, with Waters lying on his back in the end zone, Taylor stood over him, patted him on the shoulder and spoke to him.

As this was a Monday night game, Howard Cosell was on the air for ABC, and as Taylor looked down at Waters, Cosell said something like, "Well, isn't that something? The veteran Charley Taylor giving some words of encouragement to the young Cowboys defensive back."

Years later, I found out from Waters that what Taylor really said was, "Son, it'll be a long, long time before you can cover me in this league!"

That's some Hall of Fame trash talk.

## THEORY/PASS

Two basic theories exist on pass defense. One is "man" and the other is "zone."

As with our discussion of offensive line blocking, *zone* and *man* mean the same here. If it's zone, then each defensive back has an area of the field for which he's responsible. If it's man, then each defensive back and some linebackers have a receiver they are responsible for. (Usually, the linebackers cover the running backs or the tight end. You don't often see a linebacker chasing a wide receiver. If you do, something's gone very wrong on defense and the linebacker will usually see the back of the wide receiver crossing the goal line.)

Within these man and zone schemes are the same hundreds of permutations that exist in the offensive game plan. Most of them are designed to confuse the offense and conceal the exact kind of defense being played at any given moment. Watch the linebackers and the way they move right up on the line of scrimmage and then, just before the snap, move back into their coverage areas. They are trying to make the QB think a blitz (where the linebackers rush the QB in addition to the defensive linemen) is coming.

Better yet, watch the really good safeties when they come up toward the line. Often, you'll see them cheating up from their deep spot to about six yards or so off the line of scrimmage. Then, before the ball is snapped, they'll start a full speed blitz toward the QB. The great ones somehow know how to time this out so they cross the line of scrimmage a split second after the snap, avoiding a penalty for encroachment (when the defense is over the line of scrimmage at the snap).

In essence, it's a game of deception before the snap and brute force afterward. Everybody jumps around into different positions and hollers code words that may or may not mean anything. Then, the ball is snapped and for six or so seconds, it's a street fight. Ugly noises, brutal physicality, and all for the purpose of moving a little blob of leather over a few feet of grass, which sometimes is actually made of plastic.

## THEORY/RUN

Much simpler than pass defense.

1. Find guy with ball
2. Tackle him

Okay, that's a little oversimplified. But not much. When you know the run is coming—any down and one yard to go, for instance—you line up your big guys against their big guys, and whoever has the better big guys wins. The edge usually goes to the offense because they know what count the ball will be snapped on. And that half-second edge in firing out across the line of scrimmage is usually the difference.

And to show you how detailed it gets in the "trenches" where the linemen congregate, defensive linemen will watch the hand the offensive lineman opposite him is leaning down on. If the knuckles are white, it means all his weight is forward, on his hand, and he's going to fire out for a run. If the hand is a normal color, it means his weight is back, and he's going to stand up and pass block. You won't see that on your HDTV screen, no matter how big it is, but it's still fun to know.

Typically, the faster defenders will be toward the outside of the field, near the sidelines, because they have to cover more territory and cover it faster. And even the way in which they cover that territory is drilled into them time and again in practice.

When a running back gets past the line of scrimmage and is headed down the sideline, if you're a linebacker or defensive back, you can't run right, straight toward him, because he'll already be past you. You have to "take an angle." In other words, you have to run both at him and downfield at the same time, usually at about a forty-five-degree angle, so that you'll eventually get him downfield.

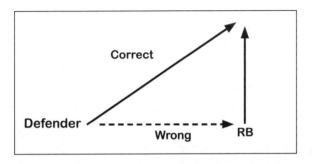

COOL THING TO SAY DURING GAME
#12

If you see a runner blow past a defensive back on the sideline, grab a handful of pretzels out of that big bowl on the table and say, "You gotta take the angles!" If the defender picks the correct angle and actually runs the ball carrier down, the proper comment is, "Nice pursuit!"

# TIME-OUT #9

Gene Stallings was, for years, an assistant coach for Tom Landry and the Cowboys. He then went on to head coaching jobs in both college and the NFL. Everybody who has ever met Gene agrees he is one of the truly fine gentlemen of the game of football. And whenever he would speak to local civic organizations, he'd repeat for his audience the speech he'd give to rookie cornerbacks on his NFL teams.

"Son, welcome to the National Football League. Let me give you a little taste of what you're in for as a cornerback at this level of the game.

"When you line up across from the receiver, one of these times you'll look up and realize that you're covering Jerry Rice, who is going to have his own wing in the Hall of Fame someday. Now...here's what happens.

"Jerry is running forwards. You're running backwards.

"Jerry knows exactly where he's going. You don't.

"Jerry knows exactly when the ball is going to be thrown. You don't.

"Jerry knows exactly where the ball is going to be thrown. You don't.

"Jerry makes five million dollars a year. You're making the league minimum.

"All we want you to do is...stop him."

Sometimes, defense it's just that easy, and just that difficult.

## DEFENSE INSTANT REPLAY

- The big guys play up front: defensive line/linebackers
- The quick guys play back: defensive backs
- The main job of the defense is to create confusion for the offense before the ball is snapped and beat the tar out of them after the ball is snapped
- Defensive linemen rush the quarterback or stop the run
- Linebackers play both run and pass defense
- Linebackers, safeties, and sometimes cornerbacks can blitz the quarterback
- There are two basic pass coverages: man and zone
- Remember the pursuit angles

# SPECIAL TEAMS: WHERE THE *FOOT* COMES BACK INTO FOOTBALL

# SPECIAL TEAMS: WHERE THE FOOT COMES BACK INTO FOOTBALL

If it's not offense or defense, then it's special teams. Basically, any time the ball is being kicked—kickoffs, punts, field goals, and points-after-touchdown—the special teams players are on the field.

And the first thing you need to know about special teams is that this is where an unknown player can "make" an NFL career. You don't generally see the ten-million-dollar-a-year guys going downfield at full speed covering kickoffs. (They don't call it the "suicide squad" for nothing!) When you have twenty-two highly trained, strong, fast, big men running at each other at full speed, things are bound to happen, and sometimes they can hurt. (Well…twenty-one men who are big, strong, and fast, really. You can't count the kickers in that group. More on that later.)

But a young player who has the guts can make his name on special teams. If you are good at covering kickoffs, at breaking through the **wedge**, clearing room for the kick return man, and tackling that return man, you've got a spot on the roster.

Conversely, if you're good at catching a kick and then running, dodging, and avoiding the other guys, you've also got a good thing going. One good kickoff return and the coaches will buy you lunch. What they're looking for are "North–South" guys. In other words, guys who catch the kick and run toward the other team's end zone. If a guy bounces around, and cuts from side to side too much, he's said to be an "East–West" guy, and he doesn't last long.

## KICKERS ARE WEIRD

Go back and read that headline again, several times.

I put it in big type for a reason. It's true! And you have to understand it. Kickers are very, very weird people.

One of the biggest changes in the NFL since the "old days" (like, before color TV) is that kickers are now of a rare, special order all their own. In those old days, the kickers were big, tough guys who played a "real" position like defensive line and, "Oh yeah, can you kick too, fella?" For over a decade, the all-time NFL scoring record was held by Cleveland's Lou "The Toe" Groza, who was also a ferocious defensive line star.

Whole generations of NFL fans have grown up not knowing what a "straight-on" kicker looks like. Well, a straight-on kicker didn't angle into the ball like today's soccer-style kickers. He ran straight at the ball and kicked it straight toward the goalpost, wearing a shoe with a special hard, square toe in it. I know this is a foreign concept for some of you younger people, but bear with an old man for a moment.

The NFL record for field goal distance is still held by a straight-on kicker who actually had a deformed foot and had to wear a specially fitted shoe: Tom Dempsey of the New Orleans

Saints for sixty-three yards (since tied by Denver's Jason Elam, for you stat freaks).

Another old-time NFL kicker, Ben Agajanian, also had a deformed foot and a special shoe. After his playing days, Ben became a respected teacher of the kicking arts. One of his pupils once asked Ben, "How can I get a kicking shoe like yours?"

"Well," Ben said, "first you get a lawnmower…"

In the mid-1960s, the Gogolak brothers, Pete and Charley, came into the NFL, the first soccer-style kickers. And unlike the hulking, straight-on guys, they were smaller. And foreign. And they didn't know much about football, American style. Stories abound of their running off the field after a successful kick shouting, "I keek touchdown!"

The last of the straight-ons, the Redskins' Mark Moseley, retired in 1986. It's been soccer style since then.

And kickers are weird in more than just the angle they take to the ball. They do strange things with their shoes. I was interviewing the Cowboys' Chris Boniol back in the nineties, and he let it slip that he broke in his kicking shoes by soaking them in near-scalding water, while his foot was inside them. This, he said, made the leather conform to the shape of his foot. But that wasn't the really weird part.

The really weird part is that Boniol wore a size nine street shoe. On the field, he wore a size seven!

"Wait a minute," I said. "You take a size nine street shoe but you wear a size seven kicking shoe? How do you get your foot in there?"

"You just kind of wedge it in."

"Doesn't it hurt? Don't your toes get all cramped?"

"Doesn't matter," Boniol said. He wanted it to feel like his shoe was just another part of his foot—one skin, so to speak. And since he was a co-holder of the record for most field goals in one game (seven—since broken), who was I to argue?

# THE KICKOFF

It's the way every game begins. The kicker puts the ball up on a tee. The kicking team lines up along either side of him on the thirty-yard line. The receiving team puts several guys about ten yards away, some more guys deep beyond them, a "wedge" of three or four guys at about the twenty, and then the kick returner around the five.

The ref blows his whistle, the kicker approaches the ball and sends it flying, and that's the last civilized moment of the game. From then on, it's street fighting.

> **COOL THING TO SAY DURING GAME**
> **#13**
>
> Whenever there is an injury time-out, a shot of a player with some blood on him, etc., give out a long sigh and then say, "It's like they say...pain and injuries are a part of the contract."

As that ball comes falling down toward the returner, ten angry, hopped up, athletic young men are bearing down on him. (The kicker is standing back, hoping somebody else makes the tackle so he doesn't have to get his uniform dirty in a futile lunge at a runner who is streaking by him for a touchdown.) The key moment in the return comes when the three or four guys who form the "wedge" link up their arms and decide which way to go. It's all been set up in advance. The return team knows how they want things to proceed. So those wedge guys move as a unit toward the onrushing defenders, and the collisions are just god-awful.

In the opening game of the 2007 season, the Buffalo Bills' Kevin Everett lowered his head as he tried to make a tackle on a kickoff. He wound up being hit in the worst possible way, on the crown of his helmet, which jammed his head down and compressed his spinal cord. He fell to the field, paralyzed. Fortunately, thanks to modern medicine, he was actually able to regain almost all of his body function over time, but it was another reminder that all these guys are really only one play away from never walking again, in the words of former Oilers center Carl Mauck. (Mauck also advanced a theory that the reason so many players get injured is that training techniques have improved to the point where players are building up musculature past the point that the skeletal systems can maintain it. They're just getting too big for their own bodies. But that's for another book.) In our fictional kickoff, nobody gets hurt like that. It's just the normal bumps and bruises.

The returner is watching his wedge, seeing how they are setting up blocks, much the same as a running back watches the offensive line set up blocks for him. But the returner is also running toward the wedge at full speed, and the judgments he makes are both instinctive and instantaneous.

And all the while, as he's watching the wedge, at least one defender is bearing straight down on it, ready to run into the middle of it and bust it up. He's the "wedge buster." He's the guy who is about to sacrifice his body…to take one for the team. In other words…he's a little nuts.

You recall our talk about pursuit angles in the section on defense? Well, it's true for kick returns, too, only more so. As the distances between the kicking team and return team are greater at the start of the play, the angles become much bigger, much quicker. If a returner gets an angle up the sideline, he can force the defenders to change their angles and miss him completely.

The one huge sin of the kickoff team is a kickoff that goes out of bounds. If it goes out of bounds in the end zone, that's good; it's called a **touchback**, and the receiving team gets the ball at their twenty-yard line. But if it goes out of bounds along the sideline, that's a penalty, and the receiving team starts with the ball on their own forty—twenty yards closer to a touchdown. And the kicker gets a very long, ugly stare from the special teams coach.

## THE PUNT

Okay, we've had a kickoff, and the offense, after a few plays, has failed to gain a first down. They are faced with fourth-and-"a bunch" somewhere farther away than the opponent's thirty-yard line. And unless it's late in the game or their coach is very gutsy, it's time to punt the ball. This is "Special Teams: Part Two."

> ### COOL THING TO SAY DURING GAME
> #### #14
>
> When the punter does launch the ball too high and too far, and you see the punt returner threading his way through huge holes for a nice return, click your tongue and announce, "He outkicked his coverage."

The punt is the special-teams play that surrenders the ball back to the other team's offense, but only after a large exchange of field position. A good punter, with a forty-yard average per kick, can put the other team way back in their own territory, an excellent exchange of field position.

The punt starts from the line of scrimmage, just like an offensive play, except that instead of a quarterback taking a snap, the ball is snapped to the punter, who stands about fifteen yards behind the line. The lineup of offensive blockers will look much different for a punt than for a run or pass play. Blockers will line up differently, some of them angled facing outward so they can try to run the other team's big guys away from the punter before he kicks. A blocked punt is a huge advantage both in field position and in attitude for the returning side.

If all goes well, the punter will kick the ball away in less than two seconds from the snap, and the punt will hang in the air at least four or more seconds, to give the coverage guys time to run downfield and stop the punt returner. (If you've ever been to an NFL game and seen punters launching the ball, it's pretty impressive. They get tremendous height and distance on the kicks, both of which are key to success in putting the other team back deep in their own territory.)

One note here is that the second-most dangerous moment in special teams play, aside from the collisions of the kickoff, is that moment when the punter has booted the ball and his kicking leg is still high in the air. At that moment, he is in a tremendously vulnerable position, obviously, and if any of the other team's guys run into him, it's called "roughing the kicker." That's a major penalty (fifteen yards) and will likely allow the punt team to keep the ball with a new first down. There's also a lesser penalty called "running into the kicker," which is just five yards and usually doesn't result in a first down. That occurs when his leg is almost back at the ground, and the potential for serious injury isn't quite as great.

The bodies flying downfield on punts go only a fraction slower and not quite as far as those kickoff coverage guys do. It's still a very dangerous part of the game, and still a place for young players to make their impact felt for the first time, both figuratively and literally.

There are subtleties to the punt; for instance, until the ball is kicked, only the two outside players on the kicking team front line can run downfield. But that's probably getting a little bit more technical than you need to worry about.

A good, high, deep kick will often force the returner to make a "fair catch," where he waves one arm back and forth over his head and essentially says, "Okay, I know I can't return this thing very far, so don't hit me. I'm just gonna catch it and stand here."

Believe it or not, a kick can go too far and too high. In that case, the ball goes so far downfield that the guys trying to stop the returner get too spread out around the field, and he can pick his way through them for a nice gain.

But, like most of the rest of the game, don't get too caught up in all this. For the punting game, just use your mental stopwatch and count off the seconds from the moment you hear the "thud" of the foot on the ball to the moment the receiver gets it.

---

**COOL THING TO SAY DURING GAME**
**#15**

When you've counted off the seconds and it hits at least four on that mental stopwatch, head for the fridge for a drink refill and, on your way out, say, "Nice hang time." (You won't miss any action because TV almost always takes a time-out after a punt.)

---

### Amazingly rare occurance

One of the least-known rules in the NFL, one even lots of TV announcers don't know, is that after you make a fair catch on a punt, and the time on the game clock expires during the play, you can choose to extend the period for one more play, but only for a field goal attempt. It's very, very rare. I've only seen it used one time in over forty years. But a hip coach who knows his rules will one day make it pay off. Picture this scenario: A punter gets a weak punt away, and the receiver fair-catches on the kicking team's side of the fifty as time expires. If you've got a field-goal kicker with a strong leg, let him give it a shot.

## THE FIELD GOAL

Okay, our offense has taken the kick and moved down to about the other team's twenty-five-yard line, but now it's fourth-and-six and they don't think they can make the first down. So, it's time for another kicking play: a field goal.

Seven yards behind the center, a holder kneels on one knee. Behind him, angled to one side, is our soccer-style kicker with the two-sizes-too-small shoe, ready to boot one through the uprights. The ball is snapped, the holder catches it and spins it around deftly so the laces aren't facing the kicker's foot, he places it on the ground at a pre-determined spot the kicker picked a moment earlier, and—boom—three points for our side.

There are very few subtle refinements to worry about here, except that the longer the field goal try, the harder it will be to make for two reasons:

1. Distance (duh!)
2. Longer kicks have to have a lower initial trajectory, which makes them easier to block. The defense will put its tallest guys on the line near the center so they can stand up and raise their long arms and be about nine feet tall in hopes of getting a piece of the ball to send it off course.

Within the past couple of seasons, a new wrinkle has been added to the field-goal game. If it's late in either half and the offense is setting up to try for a field goal, coaches for the non-kicking team will now wait until just before the snap to call a time-out and try to prey on the kicker's nerves. This has come to be known as "icing" the kicker and was first utilized by Denver head coach Mike Shanahan. It's worked maybe twice, but now, every coach tries it. But honestly, coach, the kicker has already put on a shoe two sizes too small and soaked his foot in scalding water. You really think you can mess with this guy's mind?

# PAT

Or, "Point After Touchdown." This is the kick for a single point after the six-point TD to make for the standard seven. The goal post is on the end line, ten yards behind the goal line, and the ball is placed at the two-yard line. The holder knees down seven yards behind the center, which means the ball will be snapped to the nine-yard line, making it a nineteen-yard attempt. It's pretty much automatic.

I have thought for years that the kick for a point after is *too* automatic. I think a good rule change would be to make the distance of the point-after kick depend on how far your offense had to drive for a TD. If you get the ball on your own one-yard line and have to go ninety-nine yards to score, it ought to count seven points automatically. On the other hand, if your defense gives you the ball on your opponent's one-yard line, and you only go one yard to score, you should have to try a forty-yard point-after attempt. Such a rule has not, yet, been adopted, which shows you how much influence I have on the NFL.

## OTHER TRICKS

The most notable trick in the kicking game is the **onside kick**. This is an attempt by the kicking team to barely nudge the ball so they can try to recover it for themselves. It's usually used late in the game when you're behind. The Eagles once did it on the opening kickoff of the opening game against Dallas; they scored and went on to win the game.

The tricky rule here is that for the kicking team to be able to recover the ball, it has to travel a minimum of ten yards. So the kicker has to hit a little sort of limp-footed chip shot to get the ball high, but short. Since the kickoff comes from your own thirty-yard line, you can understand the danger in an onside kick the other guys recover; they get the ball way too close to your end zone. Both the kicking and receiving teams will put their "hands" teams on the field for an obvious onside kick—guys like receivers and running backs, who are used to handling the ball and stand a better chance to catch it than, say, some 350-pound offensive tackle.

In punting, although it's a dying art, you'll occasionally see a punter try to kick the ball out of bounds deep in the other team's territory. If it goes out inside the five, he's a hero, and he's executed the perfect "coffin-corner" kick. And no, I don't know what the corner of a coffin looks like.

## SPECIAL TEAMS INSTANT REPLAY

- Kickers are weird
- Their shoes are too small
- They don't like to make tackles
- You have to be kind of crazy to play on the kickoff team
- Special teams play can be very dangerous
- If it's a kick through the uprights after a touchdown, it only counts one point
- If it's a kick through the uprights on a play from scrimmage, it counts three points
- If you kickoff out of bounds, the other team gets the ball on their own forty!
- "Icing" the kicker is nothing at all like decorating a cake

# TIME-OUT #10

Among the many perks of being an NFL player is that clothing falls from the heavens, and you get paid to wear it.

Every NFL player, from the lowly rookie to the Hall of Fame superstar, has a "shoe contract." That is, a deal with an athletic apparel manufacturer who supplies the player with shoes, warm-ups, T-shirts—all kinds of athletic gear, all for free. And the athlete gets paid, often in the millions, to wear the stuff any time he's in a game or out in public.

But it's not always what it seems.

In 1980, I was in the locker room before a game, and I saw an Oilers linebacker (who shall remain nameless) furiously drawing on his shoes with a permanent marker.

This player, like many, had his ankle tape applied over the outside of his shoes instead of inside, which obviously covered the shoe logo. And he was drawing the logo of his shoe contract on the tape.

"Wouldn't it be easier," I asked him, "to get taped inside and not have to do the artwork?"

"Yeah, it would," he replied, "but then I'd actually have to wear their damn shoes, and I hate 'em. So I wear the brand I like and do it this way instead."

And the shoe folks never found out.

# OTHER STUFF

# OTHER STUFF

It's a very complicated game, and there's lots of other stuff to learn that we don't really have time for in this book. However, just a few you should be aware of:

## THE SAFETY

A safety is a defensive scoring play determined by "impetus," meaning which player was responsible for giving the ball the momentum it needed to get into the end zone.

If you are responsible for moving the ball into your own end zone—if you run it in or fumble it in and recover, or several other things—and you get tackled holding the ball in your own end zone, or you push the ball out the back of your own end zone, that's a safety, and it counts two points for the other guys.

In addition to the embarrassment of having been tackled in your own end zone, after the safety you have to give the ball to the other team via what's called a "free kick." (A punt with nobody rushing the kicker.) Coaches don't like safeties.

On rare occasions when a team is ahead late in the game, and they are trapped deep in their own territory, the smart coach will automatically incur a safety by having his punter run the ball out of the end zone. That way, the ensuing free kick will give the other team the ball much deeper in their end of the field, and the lead will still be safe.

Many years ago, the great Minnesota Vikings defensive lineman Jim Marshall picked up a 49ers fumble and started toward the goal line. Unfortunately, it was his own goal line. Marshall ran the ball about seventy yards, the wrong way, into and out of his own end zone. The 49ers got two points for a safety and Minnesota had to kick them the ball. It's one of the most famous plays in NFL history.

## CLOCK MANAGEMENT

This is a fancy term meaning, always be aware of how much time is left and how many time-outs you have. Few things are more embarrassing than having the clock run out on you as you're hustling to get your field goal unit on the field to kick the game-winner. But, believe it or not, it happens.

As mentioned before, it actually is more effective to have your defense call time-outs late in the half to stop the clock if you're trying to get the ball back. This is because the offense has so many ways to stop the clock beside the time-out—throwing or running the ball out of bounds; running a clock play, where the QB slams the ball into the ground for an instant incomplete pass, etc. Of course, if you can leave the offense a time-out or two, that's good. But it's better to leave them no time-outs and ninety seconds than a time-out and six seconds.

## INSTANT REPLAY

Okay, send the kids out of the room, because it's rant time. I'm going to vent a little.

I'm not a fan of reviewing official's calls with TV replays. It slows the game down and it causes the officials to be second-guessed even more than they should be. No game is perfect. Let the players play. Let the refs "ref."

I think the NFL officials are the best in any sport. They make dozens of snap judgments involving huge bodies hurtling through space at rapid speeds; they interpret a very complex and lengthy rulebook; they keep order among twenty-two large men who are involved in a very emotional, hard-fought game. The number of times they blow a play that costs a game is so low, it's amazing.

(I feel a little better now. You can bring the kids back in the room. I've vented.)

Having said all that, it makes absolutely no difference what I think because replay review is here to stay, a permanent part of the game, whether I like it or not. So, let's take a few minutes to review the replay system.

Each team gets two "challenges" a game, in which they can dispute a call made on the field and appeal to replay. If the play in question is "reviewable," the ref will head over to a hooded TV monitor on the sideline and put on a headset to talk with a replay official in the press box. They will watch TV replays of the play from whatever angle the cameras saw things. If there is what the rulebook calls "indisputable visual evidence" that the call should be overturned, it is. Otherwise, the call stands as it was made on the field.

Inside the last two minutes of each half, coaches cannot instigate challenges. In the two-minute period, the replay official in the booth is the only one who can call for review. This is, obviously, to keep coaches from using replay as an extra time-out in the two-minute period.

If the team that challenged loses their challenge, they are charged a time-out, and time-outs are, as we have learned, pretty valuable. If their challenge is upheld, the call is reversed and they are not charged a time-out. (I personally think they ought to make it a lot tougher on the challenging team. You lose your challenge, the coach has to give up his office desk for a week!)

Not all plays are "reviewable." Mostly, reviewable plays relate to possession of the ball, in or out of bounds, did the ball carrier break the **plane** of the end zone and score, and some others. Let the ref sort it out when you watch a game. Just remember, it's a whole lot easier to see what happened in super slow-motion-stop-action! Anybody can make the call on tape. It's making 'em live that's tough.

## THOSE LINES ON YOUR TV SCREEN

When you watch a game on TV anymore, there are all sorts of lines all over the screen. The white lines are, of course, the yard lines, painted on the field, and they actually exist for all to see.

The colored lines, be they yellow, blue, red, whatever, are lines inserted by the TV people. The one where the ball sits obviously denotes the line of scrimmage. The one forward of the ball, in the direction the offense is moving, is an approximation of the point they need to go to make a first down. The line is not official. Indeed, the people at the stadium can't even see it. When it comes time to decide forward progress for a first down, it's still up to the refs.

Now, if we could just get them to remove all the scores and stats that crawl across the screen all game long, maybe we could see the play!

# STATS

Statistics...

- Are important (maybe)
- Tell us who did what, after a game
- Let us predict who'll do what, before a game
- Keep us occupied during the off-season
- Are fodder for arguments about whether old-time running back A was as good as current running back B

Other than that, we should always remember the story of the statistician who drowned in a river with an average depth of six inches.

There are a few stats worth keeping an eye on...

- A running back should average four yards or more per carry to be considered effective
- That same running back should gain at least 1,500 yards in 16 regular season games to be considered first-rank
- A receiver who catches one hundred balls in a season has had a great year
- A quarterback whose **quarterback rating** is higher than...wait a minute! Do you know what a "quarterback rating" is? How it's figured? Neither does almost anybody else. It's an absurd number. You know what stat matters for QBs? How many games he's won. When I was doing Cowboys broadcasts, callers to our post-game show would always complain about how Troy Aikman couldn't bring a team from behind for a victory. Well, that's because he hardly ever had to! They were always ahead. The guy won three Super Bowls in four years. What else do fans want?

## THE TWO-POINT CONVERSION

After your offense has scored a touchdown, you have the option of kicking a one-point conversion, or running another play from the defense's two-yard line for a two-point conversion.

Coaches have this chart that tells them when, in what quarter, and with what score, they should try for two. Now, keep in mind that the two-point conversion is successful only about one-third of the time, whereas the one-point kick is all but automatic. Most sane people agree that the only time you should ever consider going for two is late in the game, when you're down by more than one point.

> ### COOL THING TO SAY DURING GAME
> #### #16
>
> When your team goes for a two-point conversion, and fails, jump up out of the recliner and yell, "THEY OUGHT TO BURN THAT DAMN TWO-POINT CHART." People will admire your passion.

That chart the coaches look at is as worthless as most of the pre-game predictions I make.

If there's more odd stuff that you're not sure about, you can e-mail me at moristano@gmail.com and I'll try to set you straight.

## VITALLY IMPORTANT TRUTH

I don't care how close you are to the "Fan in your life"—friends, lovers, spouses—there is no way your big fan can tell, watching on TV, who was at fault in a particular play.

A quarterback can thread the ball through three defensive backs only to have his receiver be two feet out of position, and the result is an interception. The Fan in your life says the QB is a bum.

The coaches will say, time and again in post-game interviews, "I don't know what happened until I see the films."

What they're really talking about is videotape, but anyway, what he means is the tapes shot at the game that the coaches look at over and over and over again, in slow- and stop-motion, trying to figure out who did what.

---

**COOL THING TO SAY DURING GAME**
**#17**

When the Fan in your life is frustrated by an incomplete pass, and turns to you and says, pleadingly, "He really ran a bad route there, honey," just smile knowingly and say, "I'll have to wait for the films."

---

## TIME-OUT #11

Remember earlier, when I told you how long the memories of this game can hold on to you?

In 1967, Bart Starr and the Green Bay Packers broke my fifteen-year-old Cowboys-fan heart when they won the "Ice Bowl" NFL championship game over the Cowboys at Lambeau Field in Wisconsin.

It was thirteen below zero at kickoff, and by the time the game was won on Starr's now-legendary quarterback sneak into the end zone with almost no time left, it was nearly twenty below.

Fast-forward thirteen years. It's 1980, and I'm with the Houston Oilers Radio Network on my first visit to Lambeau Field. Before the game, I'm down on the turf watching warm-ups. I walk down to the very spot on the field where Starr snuck across for the win. At that moment, I looked up and Starr, at that time the Packers' head coach, was walking toward me.

I introduced myself and told him how he broke my heart at this spot in '67.

Starr got a very wistful smile on his face, chuckled, and walked off toward the locker room.

# WHEN YOU'RE
# AT THE GAME

# WHEN YOU'RE
# AT THE GAME

Lucky you. You must have lots of money, or neighbors with season tickets.

Anyway, most of the stuff you read here will apply at the game in person—even more so, sometimes.

At the game, try to see how the cornerbacks are lined up before the play starts, which will let you know where they want the receivers to run and where they are expecting help from.

See if you can tell whether the defense is in man or zone pass coverage. If the two safeties are hanging back, filling an area, it's likely zone. If they seem to be headed for a specific receiver, it's man. If it's zone, and you see a receiver get between two defenders deep, watch out for a touchdown.

At the stadium, you have the chance to watch the whole field.

I was at a Texas-Texas A&M game once, and A&M had a first down on their own one-yard line. They lined up in a formation with no running backs, three wide receivers, and two tight ends. At the moment the ball was snapped, I said, loud enough to be heard nearby, "Idiots!"

The A&M pass was intercepted by Texas and returned for a touchdown. People sitting around me wanted to know how I knew what was coming.

"Empty backfield, only three wideouts. Each one will have two guys on him. Get any kind of rush and it's a quick six."

They all nodded politely.

Not one of them said, "I think I'll wait for the films."

# TIME-OUT #12

And what about you, faithful football fans? What memories did I take away of you when my career in football announcing faded away? Many—indeed, some stronger than others.

1978, with the Oilers, and my first visit to Cleveland's old Municipal Stadium, also called "The Mistake by the Lake." I actually loved the place because it reminded me of old Yankee Stadium, where I grew up watching football and baseball. But the '78 game between the Oilers and Browns was one for the books.

Late in the game, the Oilers' Ken Burrough caught a TD pass in the corner of the end zone...the end zone close to the stands inhabited by the members of Cleveland's "Dog Pound." They are ardent, serious, and, frequently, inebriated fans, and when the refs ruled Burroughs' catch a TD, a hail of bottles came out of the stands toward Kenny. Liquor bottles. And they didn't get them at the concession stands.

It got so bad that the refs did something never before done in an NFL game: they played the last eight minutes or so of the game in the half of the field away from the Dog Pound. If one team had the ball and crossed the fifty-yard line, the refs turned things around so the team would go back the way they came, to keep the fans in the Pound from any more target practice.

Down on the field at the two-minute warning, waiting to go into the locker room, I made the mistake of walking down to inspect the Pound, all the while wearing my Oilers-blue jacket. It wasn't long before several bottles were heaved my way. But I managed to escape injury.

Another time with the Oilers we visited Shea Stadium, then the home of the New York Jets. This was another stadium I grew up in—box 79K, seat 4—watching the Mets play baseball. I considered it my second home—right up until I was down on the sideline again at game's end and heard a soft thud next to me on the turf. I looked down to see a spark plug lying next to me, maybe two feet away. Had it hit me, it might have done considerable damage. But my only thought was, "Who the hell brings spark plugs to a football game?"

And don't even get me started on the fans at the Oakland-Alameda County Coliseum. There were some years I thought the Raiders should let the fans play while the team watched, 'cause the fans were a lot rougher.

But hey…without the fans, you know what all this would have been? A scrimmage.

# THE REFS & THE RULES

# THE REFS & THE RULES

As mentioned earlier, the NFL game rules are very confusing, which may explain why more than a couple of the NFL game officials are attorneys in their weekday lives. Here is an actual rule, word for word, from the *2007 Official Playing Rules* of the National Football League:

> When a foul occurs during a backward pass or fumble, the basic spot of enforcement is the spot of the fumble or the spot of the backward pass. If the offensive team fouls behind the spot of the fumble or backward pass, the spot of enforcement is the spot of the foul.

Simply put: if there's a penalty on a play during which a backward pass (lateral) or a fumble occurs, the penalty will be marked off from where the fumble or lateral took place. If the offense commits a penalty behind the place where the fumble or lateral occurs, the penalty will be marked off from where the foul occurred. (Maybe not so simply put. I used five more words than the rule book!)

This is why I suggest that, as a good fan (and you are a much better fan now than you were when you first looked to these pages), you let the officials sort it all out for you. At the end of every penalty, the Referee (the official in charge) will turn on his microphone and announce to everybody what the ruling was and why.

There are seven officials on the field. They are each responsible for different areas and different things to look for. Any of them can call any penalty at any time, but they are basically to work their primary areas first.

There are two officials you'll notice more than others.

- The Referee: The guy in charge, who lines up deep behind the quarterback. He is the final authority, the chief justice, as it were. It's his crew and his ball game to run. His number-one job during a play is to see that the QB isn't roughed up too much by the defense.

- The Umpire: He's the guy who stands smack in the middle of the defense. He's forever being challenged, or actually run over, by players trying to make plays. The NFL has, at times, experimented with putting him elsewhere on the field. I don't know why anybody would think that a fifty-five-year-old guy shouldn't be standing in the midst of superb athletes in their twenties all running full speed to deck some other guy. A good runner or receiver can actually use the umpire as an extra blocker if he's in that area of the field.

You'll also note, from time to time, the official called the "Head Linesman" bringing in the "chain gang" from the sidelines. This is the ten-yard-long chain that is used to measure each series of downs. If the ball is close to the distance needed for a first down, the ref will call in the chains, and they'll measure to see if it's a first or not. With all the computers, replays, and high-tech stuff in football today, they still make this important measurement with a device made from stuff they bought at The Home Depot!

## PENALTIES

The penalties the officials mete out are basically broken into three groups:

**Major Penalties**: For dangerous things that might lead to ugly injury. These penalties are fifteen yards. Some of the "major" major penalties include

- Clipping: blocking below the waist from behind
- Interfering with fair catch
- Hands to the face: smacking a player with the open palm on the side of the helmet; also called "ringing the bell"
- Illegal hands to the face, head, or neck with palm
- Face mask: pulling the face mask (obviously to prevent neck injuries)
- Roughing the kicker: running into a kicker while his leg is still in a vulnerable, raised position
- Unnecessary roughness: (as opposed to the necessary kind) tackling a runner who is out of bounds, or executing a "crack-back" block, which is a way for receivers to come down at full speed on a defender and smash into the side of the legs when the defender isn't able to prevent it
- Unsportsmanlike conduct: abusive or insulting language or behavior toward officials; taunting (see *Monty Python and the Holy Grail*)
- Many others

**Disqualification Penalties:** These are always fifteen-yard penalties plus disqualification from the game for the offending player;

- Flagrant roughing of kicker or passer
- Flagrant unsportsmanlike conduct
- Using the helmet as a weapon

**Minor Penalties:** These penalties are five yards. Some minors include

- False Start: the offense jumping across the line of scrimmage before the snap
- Encroachment: the defense jumping across the line of scrimmage before the snap
- Delay of game
- **Neutral zone** infraction
- Ineligible player downfield on pass or kick

(Note: The five-yard penalties that occur before the ball is ever snapped, like offside or encroachment, drive coaches crazy. There is no excuse for having four or five of these in a game.)

**Middle Penalties:** Ten yards long. They include

- Pass interference by the offense (pass interference by the defense moves the ball to the spot where the foul occurred)
- Batting a loose ball toward opponents goal line

One penalty, pass interference on the defense, gives the offense the ball at the spot where the infraction took place. Occasionally, if a cornerback is badly beaten on a pass play, and he knows it, he'll intentionally interfere with the receiver to prevent a TD. The offense gets the ball at the spot of the foul or, if the interference occurs in the end zone, at the one-yard line.

Once close to the end zone, penalties begin to be marked off in increments of half the distance to the goal line. For instance, from the four-yard line, encroachment on the defense would put the ball in the end zone, so a two-yard penalty is marked off instead.

While I don't believe it's ever occurred in an NFL game, there are a couple of very rare situations where the referee can actually award points to a team. This would be if a ball carrier is streaking downfield for a sure touchdown, with no defender near him, and a player from the other team comes off the bench and tackles him. This is called a "palpably unfair act," and it's at the ref's discretion to go ahead and award a touchdown. (It did happen in the 1954 Cotton Bowl college game, when an Alabama player named Tommy Lewis came off the bench and tackled Rice RB Dickie Maegle as he streaked toward the 'Bama end zone. The ref awarded Rice the TD.)

## A WORD ABOUT REFS

I think the NFL officials are the best in any sport: consistently correct and always on top of the play.

Watch when they replay a close call. Look to see how many of the officials are right there, eyes on the play, ready to make the call. And tell the Fan in your life for me that I guarantee you, no matter how many times that fan has said, "Hell, I could have made the call better than that!"...*No, they couldn't.* The size and speed of the players, and the tension involved in each of these plays is not to be believed. I've seen it from the same angle the refs do, on the sideline, up close. To be able to judge if the receiver got both feet down in bounds, while also keeping possession of the ball, is a huge challenge. There is little, or nothing that goes on down on that field that the average fan could deal with. Trust me!

These officials have been calling football for decades at the high school and college levels, and, just as with the players, only the best make it to the NFL. But they have the added burden of having to make certain that all the testosterone that's flooding the NFL field doesn't get out of hand. They have to maintain order and make certain that players who are much bigger, younger, and stronger respect their every judgment.

Or, as they like to say, football officials have to start out perfect the first day, and get better from then on!

## OVERTIME

Every so often, a game ends as a tie after four quarters. Except, it doesn't really end. If both teams have the same point total, we have another coin toss, just like at the start of the game, and we play **overtime**. Just about the same rules as a regular quarter, except that the first team to score, by any method, wins. In regular season, if a fifteen-minute overtime quarter is scoreless, then the game is finally a tie. But in the playoffs, you keep playing overtime periods until somebody wins, because one team always has to win a playoff game and advance to the next round. That's the great thing about the NFL playoffs. One game. Win, and you go on. Lose, and you go home.

# TIME-OUT #13

What's in a name? Well, when Shakespeare wrote that line, not too much. I mean, sure, you might win Juliet or some such.

But in today's big sports biz, a name can be worth multi-millions of dollars. Meaning, the naming rights to a new stadium.

It was one of my biggest crusades when I called games that I would never refer to a stadium by its paid name if it had an original name, like Soldier Field in Chicago, or San Francisco's Candlestick Park. People would always tell me, "But, Mark, it's now called First National Trans-American Continental Banking Plaza Stadium at the Meadows."

"No! It's Candlestick Park! And if that bank that bought the naming rights wants their name used on our broadcast, they can darn well come to our station and buy some commercial time."

People scoffed at me. I was an object of ridicule. Children would point at me and laugh.

And then…vindication! NBC was televising a NASCAR race, the naming rights of which had been sold to Lowe's hardware. But NBC's announcers continued to use only the old, traditional name of the race. When Lowe's complained, NBC said, "You want us to use your name…buy ad time." And they did!

Somebody asked me what I'd call Texas Stadium if Jerry Jones, the Cowboys owner, sold the naming rights to it.

"Whatever Jerry wants me to call it."

# POST-GAME

# POST-GAME

Okay, the game is over, the living room has been cleaned up, and you've impressed the heck out of everyone with your newfound knowledge of football. Now what?

Live a normal life for six days, until the next game rolls around. Read the sports page if you want, watch the NFL Network for some inside information—but don't let the game consume you.

Unless you make your living from it, like the players and coaches do—or like the broadcasters do—just use it as an excuse to get together with friends for some fun and socialization.

Don't take the game seriously. It's a game. You can follow the coaching rule, which says the players are allowed to be elated after a win, or upset after a loss, for only twenty-four hours, and then it's on to next week.

The day after the Boston Red Sox lost the 1986 World Series to the New York Mets, I said on the air that the Sox had to take the world's longest fifty-minute plane ride back to Boston.

I got off the air and was told I had a phone call. I picked up the phone.

"Hello?"

"Mahhhk!"

"You're from Boston, aren't you?"

"Yes, and I want to tell you I'm so angry that you said the Red Sox would have to take a long flight. They did great. They were tremendous."

"Yes, I agree. But I took two flights just like that with the Houston Oilers after they lost the AFC championship to Pittsburgh and missed out on the Super Bowl. And it's a terrible feeling."

"Mahhhhk, this series has been so difficult for me. I haven't been able to sleep. I haven't been eating."

"Let me ask you a question, ma'am." (Yes, it was a woman fan!) "When you go to see a movie you've really been looking forward to, and it's not as good as you'd hoped, do you get this upset?"

"No, of course not."

"Well, that World Series was entertainment. Just like a movie. It's a game. If you're not making you're living from it…don't let it control your life."

She thought for a moment.

"You may be right," she said.

At least we parted friendly.

And—one final thought—you should always heed the words of former Cowboys running back Duane Thomas. Duane was a player of great talent, but in the seventies, he was also a man of the most confusing behavior patterns. He spent one entire season not talking to anybody: teammates, media—nobody.

Anyhow, when the Cowboys and Thomas reached the Super Bowl that season, a reporter asked Duane how it felt to play in the "ultimate game."

"If it's the ultimate game," Duane said, "how come they're playing another one next year?"

---

**ULTIMATE, ALWAYS APPLICABLE, COOL THING TO SAY DURING GAME**

Whether it's your nephew's peewee game or the Cowboys and Steelers slugging it out in the Super Bowl—any time your team gives up a fumble or an interception, slowly shake your head from side to side and mumble, "**Turnovers**, (long pause) **turnovers**, (longer pause) **turnovers.**"

---

# GLOSSARY

**audible.** Code words called by the quarterback at the line of scrimmage that actually change the play to be run. This usually happens when the QB sees that the defense is in perfect position to stop the play originally called and land the QB staring at the sky while flat on his back.

**blitz.** When the defense sends more than the four defensive linemen chasing after the quarterback when he drops back to pass. A blitz can come from linebackers or defensive backs. It's a gamble, because if they don't get to the quarterback, there's now a gap somewhere on the field for a receiver to find and make lots of yards.

**blind side.** The quarterback's left side if he's right-handed, or vice versa. When the QB is looking downfield to pass, he obviously can't see behind him. Any onrushing defender coming on the QB's blind side can do some serious damage.

**blocking.** Basically, the football equivalent of getting in the other guy's way. Linemen, running backs, wide receivers, sometimes even quarterbacks block. Usually, though, just linemen and running backs. There are many kinds of blocks, some very blatant and potentially dangerous. Remember, offensive players block; defensive players tackle.

**clock play.** During the two-minute drill, when the QB wants to stop the clock without using a time-out, he simply throws the ball straight into the ground as soon as he gets it from the center.

**defense.** The unit on the field opposing the offense. The defense tries to keep the offense out of the end zone that the defense is defending.

**down.** (1) An offensive play. In each series, the offense has four downs (plays) to make ten yards, after which they are awarded another four downs to make another ten yards, etc.; (2) when whoever has the ball is tackled, he is said to be "down."

**draft.** The annual gathering where pro teams get to select the rights to college players and pay them millions of dollars for skills they've yet to demonstrate as professionals.

**drive.** The series of offensive plays that runs from the moment the offense takes possession of the ball to the moment they either score or give the ball back to the other team.

**eligible receiver.** Any offensive player positioned so that he's not one of the five interior offensive linemen, or the quarterback (except from the T formation), is eligible to go downfield and catch passes.

**end zone.** The ten-yard space at each end of the field with the goal line at one end and an end line at the other. This is the space you want to get into. Get the ball in to the other guy's end zone and it's a touchdown. The goal posts are on the end line of the end zone, ten yards behind the goal line.

**field goal.** When the offense has fourth down and the end zone isn't close enough to go for a touchdown, it's time for a field goal. A holder kneels down seven yards behind the center, takes the snap, places the ball on the ground and a soccer style kicker knocks it up through the uprights for three points.

**field position.** The area of the field where the offense takes possession of the ball. If you get the ball on your own ten-yard line, that's *bad* field position. If you get the ball on the other team's ten-yard line, that's *great* field position.

**fumble.** When an offensive player drops the ball and the defense recovers it. Or, when he gets smashed silly, the ball falls out of his hands, and the defense recovers it.

**hash marks.** A series of marks the length of the field, between every five-yard line incremental marker. The hash marks are as far apart as the upright portions of the goal posts, so the hash marks are farther apart in high school and college, where the goal posts are wider than they are in the NFL.

**hole.** The space between two linemen on the line of scrimmage where the running back is supposed to run through.

Also called a "gap" at times, although nothing in khaki is available at these gaps.

**interception.** One of the dreaded turnovers. When your QB throws a pass caught by somebody on the other team—*bad*. When their QB throws a pass caught by somebody on your team—*good*.

**intentional grounding.** Major penalty called on the quarterback when he deliberately throws an incomplete pass to avoid a yardage loss from a potential sack. If he intentionally grounds the ball while standing in the end zone, it's a safety, and the other team gets two points plus the ball. If it happens between the goal lines, it's a ten-yard penalty and loss of down.

**kickoff.** At the start of the game, the ref tosses a coin, the visiting team captain calls heads or tails, and whoever wins the toss gets to choose to kickoff or receive a kickoff. The kickoff comes from your thirty, and you don't want the returning team to take it past their own twenty. The kickoff also starts off the second half and occurs after each offensive scoring play, with the team that scored kicking off to the other side.

**line of scrimmage.** The yard line on the field where the ball rests to start a play. The offense lines up on one side of the line of scrimmage and the defense on the other. The width of the ball along the line of scrimmage is called the **neutral zone** and is no man's land, empty, barren, stay out of it. The center, who snaps the ball to the quarterback, is the obvious exception, as he has to reach into the zone to snap the ball.

**man.** (1) On offense, man blocking means each lineman takes on one man near him; (2) on defense, man defense means a defender is responsible for only one receiver, and follows that man wherever he goes; (3) the QB... he's *the* man!

**man in motion.** One, and only one, player from the offense may be moving when the center snaps the ball to the quarterback, but only parallel to, or away from, the line of scrimmage.

**neutral zone.** The width of the football along the entire line of scrimmage. Nobody may line up in the neutral zone; otherwise, it's a five-yard penalty.

**nickel.** When the defense puts in a fifth defensive back, he's called the "nickel" back. Five backs. Fives cents in a nickel. Get it?

**offense.** The eleven players on the field with possession of the football.

**onside kick.** From a kickoff-type formation, the kicking team will try to kick the ball ten yards and recover it before the receiving team can get to it. If it doesn't go ten yards, that's a penalty and the receiving team automatically gets the ball. A very risky play.

**overtime.** If the game is tied at the end of four quarters, you head into overtime. In the NFL it's played just like a fifth quarter. The first team to score wins. If no team scores in the fifteen-minute overtime in regular season play, the game ends in a tie. In the playoffs, there can be no ties. You play until one team scores. The longest game ever played was a playoff game between Kansas

City and Miami in 1971, at eighty-two minutes and forty seconds. Miami won in the second overtime on a field goal. Overtime in college is run differently. Each team gets at least one series until one team winds up ahead, the plays are run from the twenty-five-yard line. And no, nobody gets time-and-a-half for overtime.

**PAT (Point After Touchdown).** An extra, untimed play run from the two-yard line after a touchdown. It's usually a kick, like a field goal, but it counts only one point (but see **two-point conversion**). However, any blocked kicks, fumbles, or interceptions may not be returned by the defense.

**plane.** An imaginary line that extends straight up from the front edge of the goal line, to infinity. If the football, in the possession of an offensive player, breaks any part of that plane, it is a touchdown.

**play-action.** A pass play that starts off with a well-faked handoff to a runner, to make the defense think a run is coming and draw the linebackers and defensive backs in a step or two. This gives the receivers a chance to escape downfield.

**pocket.** The semicircle of protection formed by the offensive line around the QB as he attempts to pass.

**point of attack.** Coach talk for the place the offense wants to try to open a hole in the defense to run the ball through.

**punt.** When it's fourth down and you're too far away to kick a field goal, you punt the ball back to the other guys. Your punter stands fifteen yards behind the line, takes a long snap, and lets loose a booming kick, which ought to hang in the air at least four seconds to give the cover guys a chance to get downfield and chase the punt returner.

**quarter.** The basic divisions of time in football. In pro football, a game is four fifteen-minute quarters. In high school and college, the quarters are shorter.

**quarterback rating.** A mathematical formula devised by the same people who brought you the sub-prime mortgage crisis, which is supposed to be an accurate measure of a quarterback's ability. It is impossible to understand, even for veteran football people. The next time the Fan in your life mentions it, chuckle to yourself and change the subject to subatomic particles or some other, simpler topic.

**red zone.** The area inside the other team's twenty-yard line. Once you move the ball into the red zone, you want to come out with some points. At least a field goal (three) and hopefully a TD (six, plus the one-point PAT kick, for a total of seven). The winning teams have excellent red zone percentages, meaning the number of points they take away with them for each visit to the red zone.

**route.** Short for pass-route, the specific patterns that receivers run downfield to try to get free of any defenders so the quarterback can pass the ball to them.

**sack.** (1) Tackling the QB behind the line of scrimmage while he's attempting to pass; (2) headgear worn by fans of teams having lousy seasons, so nobody will know they are actually at the game.

**safety.** When the offense is guilty of being tackled with the ball in their own end zone, or being responsible for the ball going out of the end of their own end zone, the defense gets a two-point safety. Plus, the offense then has to free kick the ball back to the defense. (Not to be confused with the position of safety, which is a defensive back who is stationed well back in the defensive alignment.)

**scouting combine.** The annual meeting of coaches, executives, and college players where the players run races, jump through hoops, lift weights, and show off all their skills short of actually playing the game. The main tests are the forty-yard dash, the bench press, and the vertical jump.

**shotgun formation.** Nothing to do with an unplanned wedding. This is when the quarterback stands five to eight yards behind the center, who sort of passes the ball to the quarterback upside down between his legs. This formation gives the quarterback a chance to see more of the defense quicker. The center, however, mostly sees the quarterback upside down.

**snap.** The center passing the ball backward between his legs to start the play.

**special teams.** The plays that involve kicking or returning kicks. See **punt**, **field goal**, **kickoff**, and **PAT**.

**spread formations.** High-octane formations where receivers and running backs line up way outside, toward the sidelines. This "spreads" the defenders wider apart and creates more open areas for things to happen for the offense.

**Super Bowl.** (Do I really need to define this for you?) The National Football League Championship Game. The biggest sports event in America. At halftime of this game, toilets all over the nation flush at once. The game got its name when Lamar Hunt, owner of the Kansas City Chiefs, saw his daughter playing with a "Super Ball." The league had been looking for a good name for the game, which, in its early stages, was called the "AFL-NFL World Championship Game."

**T formation.** When the quarterback lines up directly behind the center and the play starts with the center handing (snapping) the ball to the quarterback backward through his legs.

**tackling.** What the defense must do to the guy with the ball. Get him either out of bounds, or on the ground with at least one knee touching down. Sometimes it's as simple as a little shove; sometimes it's a vicious, career-ending, horrible collision. Former pro player and coach Carl Mauck was fond of saying that "Pro football players are always one play away from never walking again." The unspoken truth about the violence of the game is always in the mind, but rarely given a voice.

**touchback.** A kickoff or punt that goes out of bounds or dies in the receiving team's end zone. The receiving team gets the ball on their own twenty-yard line.

**touchdown.** When you push the ball across your opponent's goal line. Counts six points.

**turnover.** Not a pastry. Anything that turns the ball over to the other team. A fumble, an interception. Very, very costly. Coaches hate turnovers.

**two-minute drill.** The special set of plays offenses run when there are two minutes or less to go in a half. The object is to run the plays as quickly as possible, with as little of the clock run off as possible. A good two-minute offense can move the ball half the field in forty-five seconds and score.

**two-point conversion.** After you've scored a touchdown, you have the option to kick a PAT for one point or, if you need more, you can run a play from the two-yard line. You can either run or pass and, if you reach the end zone, get two points. If you fail on either the one or two point conversion, you get only the six points for the touchdown.

**wedge.** (1) The four men right in front of the kickoff returner who link their arms and try to steamroll a path for the returner; (2) in Northern cities, what they call a hero sandwich.

**zone.** (1) On offense, zone blocking means all the linemen block in the same general direction, sort of like a human plow, sweeping away all in their path; (2) on defense, the certain area of the field assigned to a defender to cover pass plays.